ERRATUM
Light Breaks Where No Sun Shines ....
Changes in Acknowledgements

P.36	Bottom left image by Zena James
P.42	Image on bottom right by Brian Derrick
P.45	Image by Brian Leonard
P.48	Image by Zena James
P.54	Top image by Marina Evans
P.68	Second image on the right by Ursula Calvin-Thomas
P.70	Image by Rita Williams
P.72	Bottom right image by Zena James
P.76	Middle image by Brian Leonard
P.79	Image by Hilary Ferris
P.82	Top image by Robert Wyman
P.83	Top image by Beryl Clothier (top)
P.83	Bottom left image by Lorna Thornton
P.87	Image by Anthony Rowlands

Light breaks where no sun shines ...

new images of Dylan Thomas' poetry

Thanks to
Brian Gaylor, Phil Cope, Darren Dobbs, David Woolley, Sean Keir,
Adult Learning Section, City and County of Swansea, Gorseinon College, Swansea, Swansea Camera Club,
Swansea Institute of Higher Education and the many people who took part.
Cover image by Jackie Davies

The Project was funded by
the City & County of Swansea Culture & Recreation Department,
Dylan Thomas Centre & Leisure Promotions
and the Arts Council of Wales.

a

centre
Tŷ Llên Publications
production

01792 463980

dylanthomas.lit@swansea.gov.uk

www.dylanthomasfestival.com

ARIENNIR GAN Y LOTERI
LOTTERY FUNDED

CEFNOGI CREADIGRWYDD
CYNGOR CELFYDDYDAU CYMRU
THE ARTS COUNCIL OF WALES
SUPPORTING CREATIVITY

ISBN - 0-9533865-7-0

© October 2003

light breaks where no sun shines ...

new Images of Dylan Thomas' poetry

This book, and the exhibition that it accompanies, is the result of a participatory project organised by the City and County of Swansea as part of the major Dylan Thomas 50 Schools and Community initiative run by the Dylan Thomas Centre to commemorate the fifty years since Dylan Thomas' death.

Light Breaks was designed to increase the awareness of Dylan Thomas' ability to create vibrant visual imagery in the mind of his readers. Local people were encouraged to produce work based upon their own interpretations of Thomas' writing. An avalanche of inspiring responses came from a wide range of individuals, organisations and groups including Swansea Adult Learners, Swansea Camera Club, and the students of Swansea Institute and Gorseinon College, with the ages of the artists ranging from 16 to over 80.

All the participants were given a completely open brief as to the selection of writing and the method of reflecting and interpreting it in a visual image. The range of these translations from text to image and the skills shown in the final images are amazing. This publication and exhibition has demonstrated powerfully how readers see Thomas' poetic imagery in vastly differing ways and how their choice of mediums can also influence the final work. It was initially pointed out to the artists that there could not be a wrong entry, as whatever they choose to enter was a reflection of their own thoughts and responses, and, therefore, worthy of consideration.

It is hoped that viewers of this book and visitors to the exhibition will themselves find renewed inspiration to look into the fathomless writing of Dylan Thomas and perhaps find their own visual images to compliment his wonderful words.

Brian Gaylor FRPS
Light Breaks Project co-ordinator

Unknown

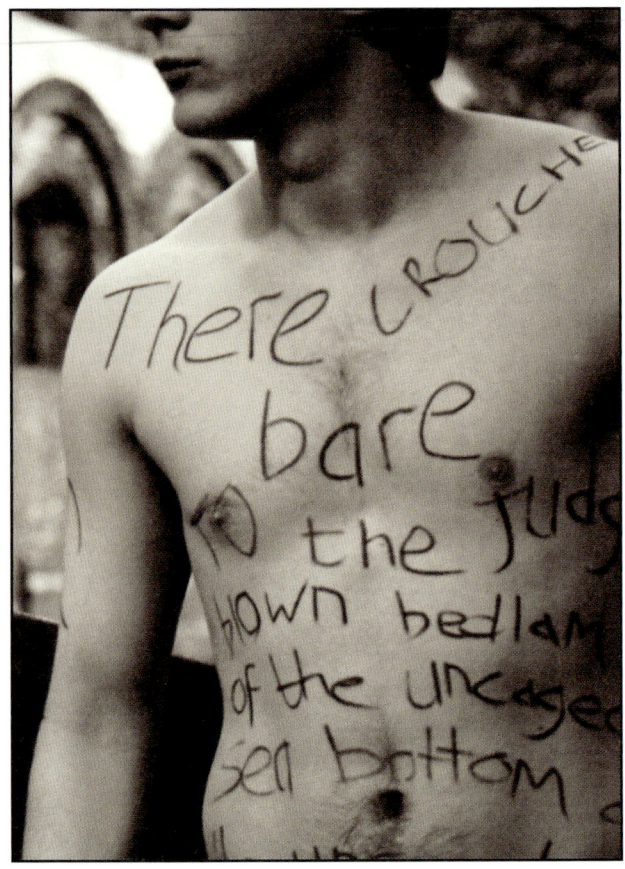

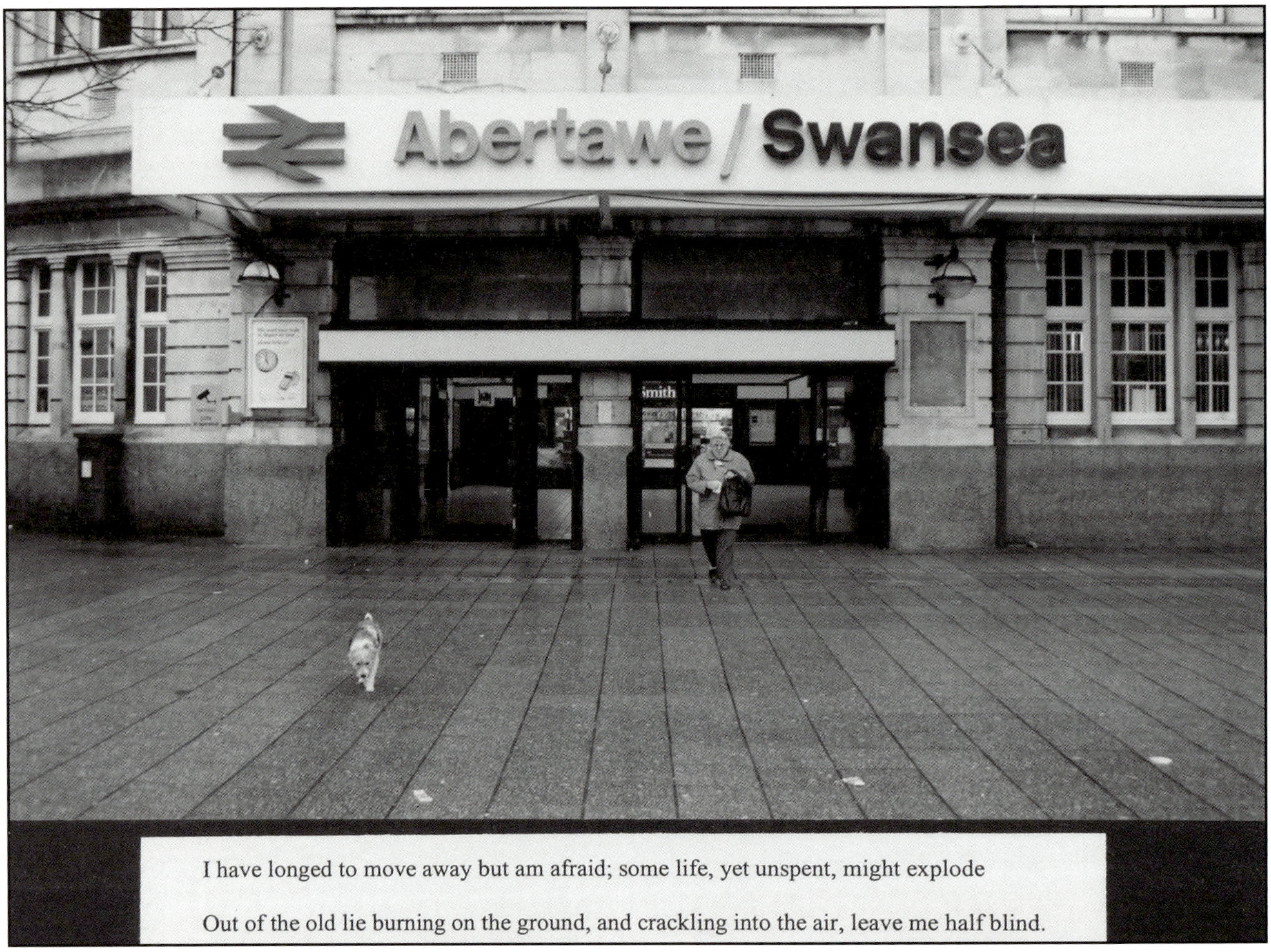
Abertawe / Swansea
I have longed to move away but am afraid; some life, yet unspent, might explode
Out of the old lie burning on the ground, and crackling into the air, leave me half blind.

Lorna Thornton

There
bare
the
bedlam
of the
sea bottom

Zena James

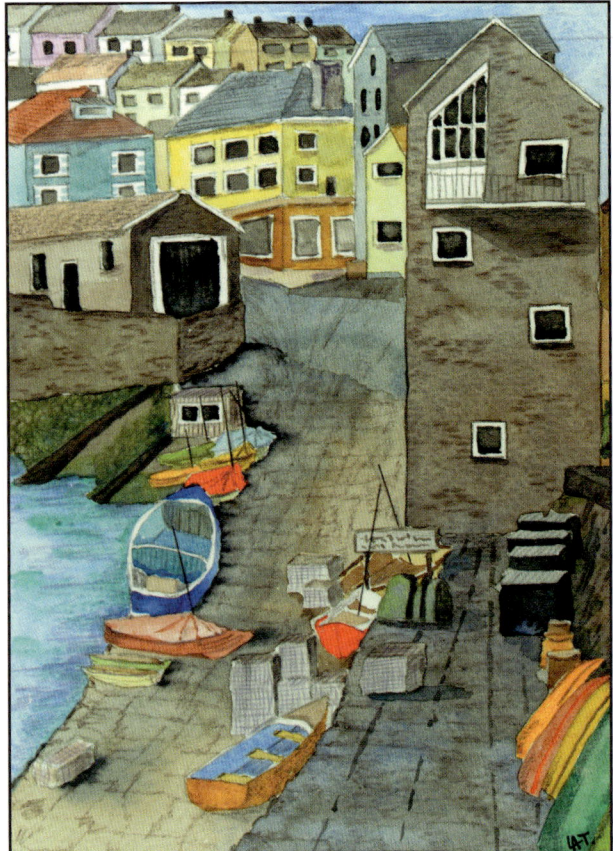

Roy Kneath

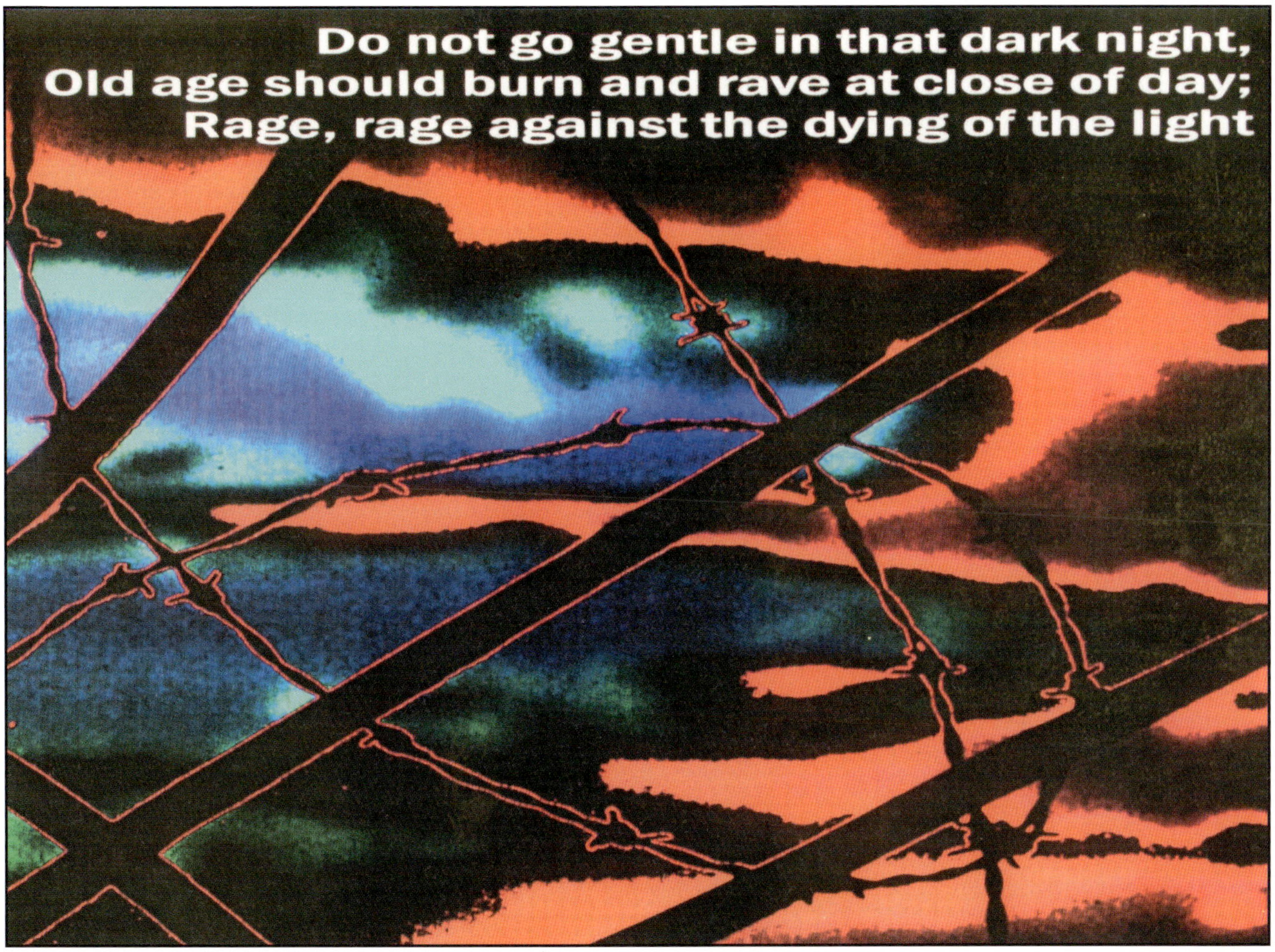
Do not go gentle in that dark night,
Old age should burn and rave at close of day;
Rage, rage against the dying of the light

I see the boys of summer
I see the boys of summer in their ruin
as Sunlight paints the shelling of their heads

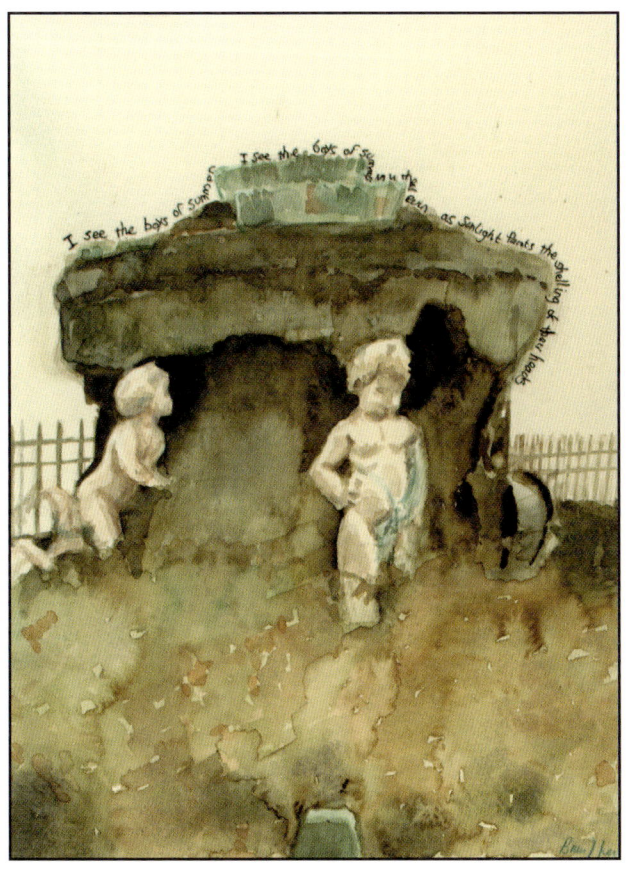

Brian Leonard

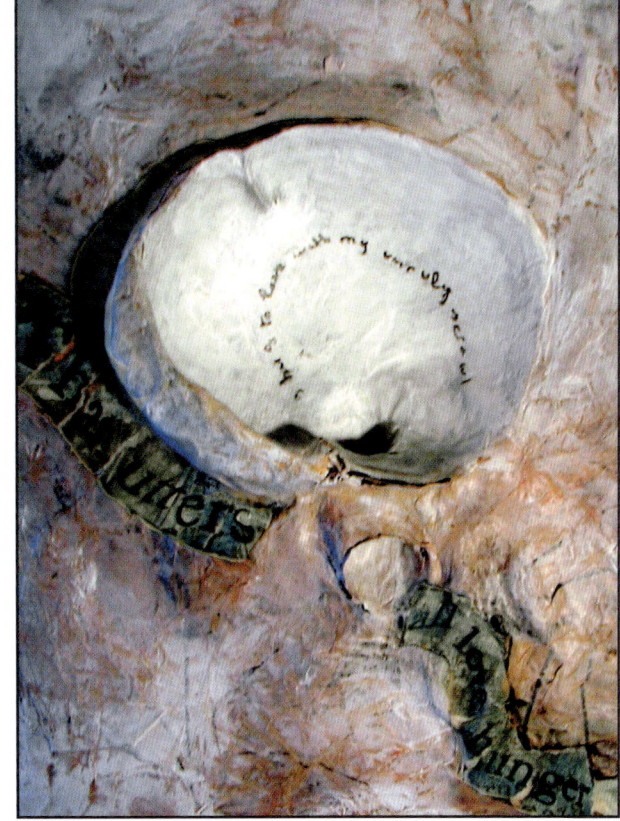

Jackie Davies

Vision and Prayer

Who
Are you
Who is born
In the next room
So loud to my own
That I can hear the womb
Opening and the dark run
Over the ghost and the dropped son
Behind the wall thin as a wren's bone?
In the birth bloody room unknown
To the burn and turn of time
And the heart print of man
Bows no baptism.
But dark alone
Blessing on
The wild
Child.

To the burn and turn of time

Jackie Davies

Rita Ford

Judith Roeder

I dived my beggar arm
Days deep in her breast that wore no heart

THE FORCE THAT THROUGH THE GREEN FUSE

Fraser Lawson

Lisa Ann Tallis

Kate Adams

Throw wide to the wind the gates of the wondering boat

All night in the unmade park   After the railings and shrubberies

YOU WHO BOW DOWN TO CROSS AND ALTAR,

Gareth Brooks

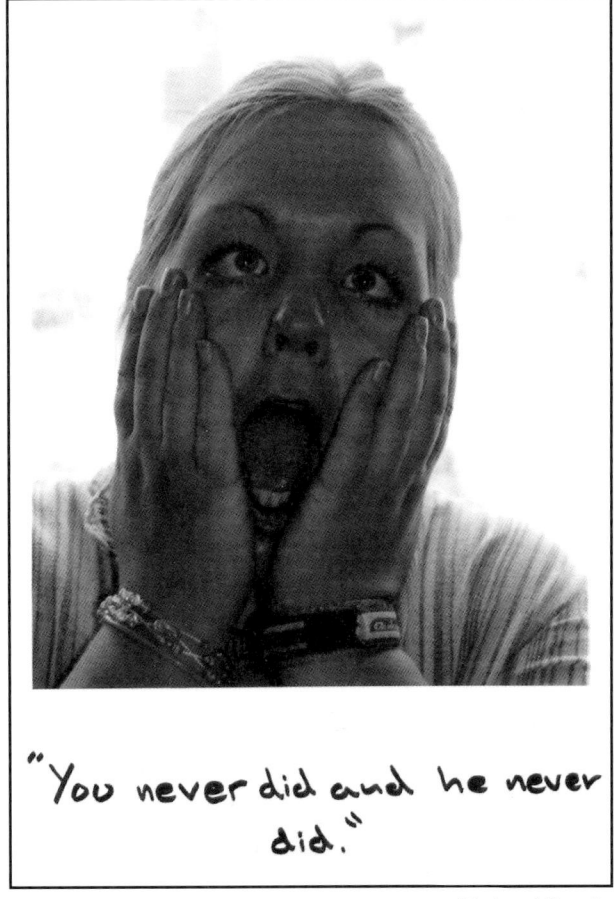

"You never did and he never did."

Richard Booth

the force
that through
the green
fuse

Jackie Davies

10

---From Harbour and Neighbour Wood
and the Mussel Pooled and the Heron
Priested Shore ---

Michael J Bent

11

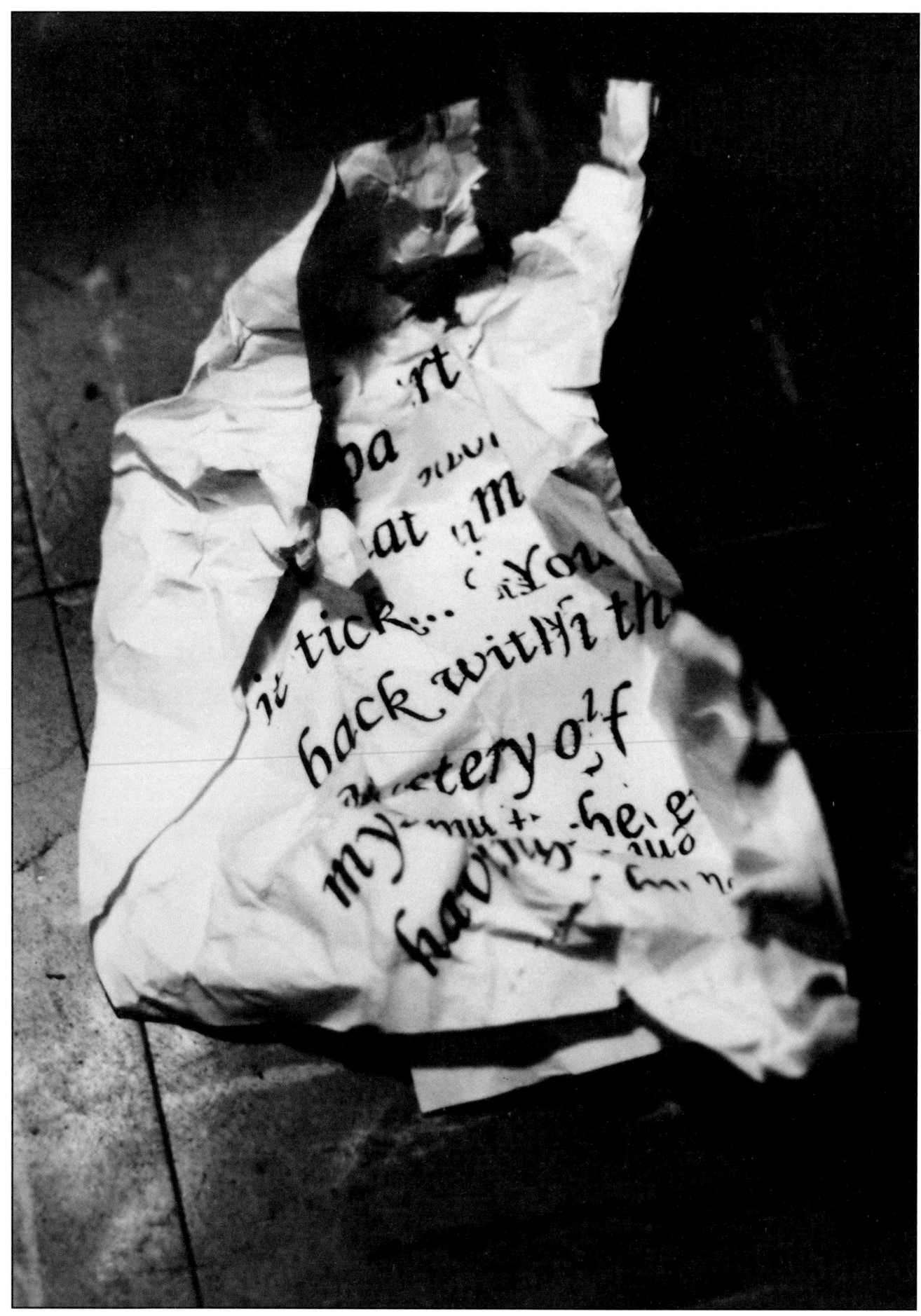

Unknown

Tracey Dobson

...walking the nightmarish room

Unknown

Dear Gwalia! I know there are Towns lovelier than ours, And fairer hills and loftier far, And groves more full of flowers, And boskier woods more blithe with spring And bright with birds' adorning, And sweeter bards than I to sing Their praise this beauteous morning. By Cader Idris, tempest-torn, Or Moel yr Wyddfa's glory, Carnedd Llewelyn beauty born, Plinlimmon old in story, By mountains where King Arthur dreams, By Penmaen-mawr defiant, Llaregyb Hill a molehill seems, A pygmy to a giant. By Sawdde, Senny, Dovey, Dee, Edw, Eden, Aled, all, Taff and Towy broad and free, Llyfnant with its waterfall, Claerwen, Cleddau, Dulais, Daw, Ely, Gwili, Ogwr, Nedd, Small is our River Dewi, Lord, A baby on a rushy bed. By Carreg Cennen, King of time, Our Heron Head is only A bit of stone with seaweed spread Where gulls come to be lonely. A tiny dingle is Milk Wood By Golden Grove 'neath Grongar But let me choose and oh! I should Love all my life and longer To stroll among our trees and stray In Goosegog Lane, on Donkey Down, And hear the Dewi sing all day, And never, never leave the town.

may you have a strong foundation
may your heart always be joyful,
may you stay forever young.

when the winds of changes shift,
may your song always be sung.
Dylan Thomas – Bob Dylan – KB '03

This bread I break was once the oat,

Tom Chapman

Tracey Dobson

Unknown

Lisa Ann Tallis

Under the mile off moon we trembled listening to the sea sound flowing like blood from the loud wound

Zena James

Zena James

Brian Gaylor

When like a running grave, time tracks you down

Captain Cat
The retired blind sea captain

Never such sea as any
that swamped the decks
of his S.S. Kidwelly.

Roy Kneath

Irene Thomas

Jackie Davies

Dennis Russ

Jack Thorpe

Lisa Ann Tallis

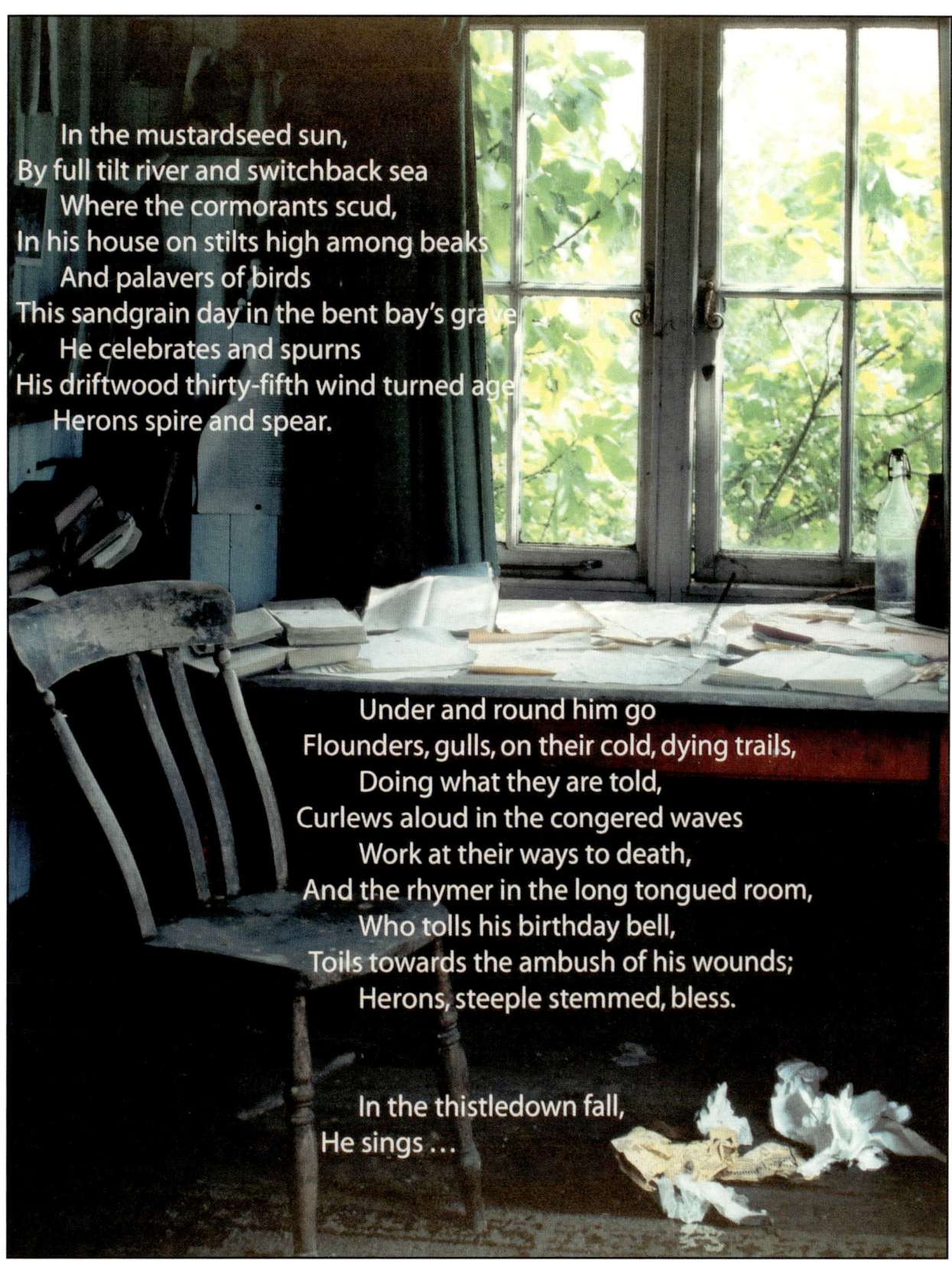

In the mustardseed sun,
By full tilt river and switchback sea
    Where the cormorants scud,
In his house on stilts high among beaks
    And palavers of birds
This sandgrain day in the bent bay's grave
    He celebrates and spurns
His driftwood thirty-fifth wind turned age
    Herons spire and spear.

            Under and round him go
    Flounders, gulls, on their cold, dying trails,
            Doing what they are told,
    Curlews aloud in the congered waves
            Work at their ways to death,
    And the rhymer in the long tongued room,
            Who tolls his birthday bell,
    Toils towards the ambush of his wounds;
            Herons, steeple stemmed, bless.

            In the thistledown fall,
    He sings ...

Phil Thomas

23

Jackie Davies

John Davies

Dave Condon

Brian Gaylor

I am going into the darkness of the darkness for ever.   I have forgotten that I was ever born.

And Steam Comes Screaming Out Of Her Navel

Dai Evans

Then you cried like a baby and said you had nowhere to go but the grave.

Mr and Mrs Cherry Owen

Roy Kneath

Michael J Bent

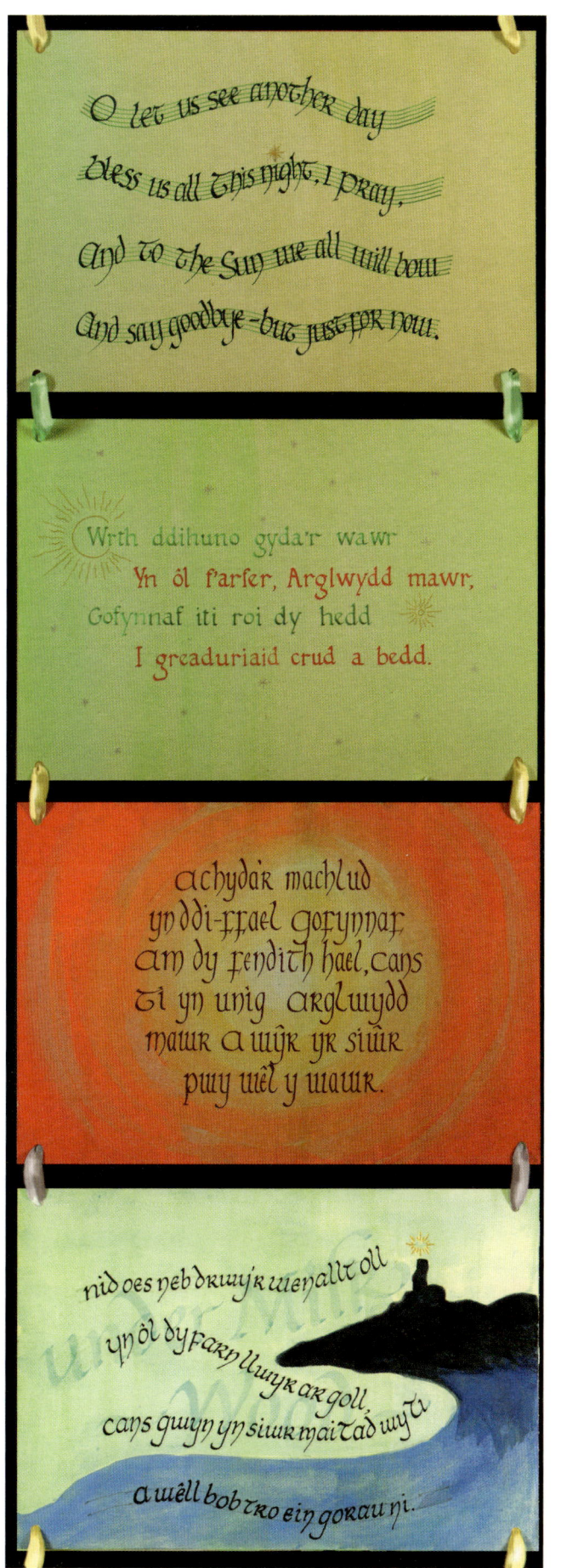

O let us see another day
bless us all this night, I pray,
And to the Sun we all will bow
And say goodbye – but just for now.

Wrth ddihuno gyda'r wawr
Yn ôl f'arfer, Arglwydd mawr,
Gofynnaf iti roi dy hedd
I greaduriaid crud a bedd.

A chyda'r machlud
yn ddi-ffael gofynnaf
Am dy fendith hael, cans
Ti yn unig Arglwydd
mawr a ŵyr yr siŵr
pwy wêl y wawr.

nid oes neb drwy'r wenallt oll
yn ôl dy farn llwyr ar goll,
cans gwyn yn siŵr mai tad wyt ti
a wêl bob tro ein gorau ni.

The Judith Porch group

THE
Reverend Jenkins
PRAYER

Every morning when I wake,
DEAR LORD
a little prayer I make,
O please to keep
THY LOVELY EYE
On all poor creatures born to die.

We are not wholly bad or good
who live our lives under
milk-wood
and thou, I know, wilt be the first
to see our best side, not our worst

The Judith Porch group

Bolting the door of the night with her arm. Her plume straight in the mazed bed. She deludes the heaven-proof house with entering clouds

LOVE IN THE ASYLUM--Dylan Thomas

Dave Williams

> Grief with dishevelled hands tear out the alter ghost <

> Time marks a black aisle kindle from the brand of ashes <

> And a firewind kill the candle <   -   > Dylan Thomas <

Dyffrig Gill

29

Lie Still
Sleep Becalmed

Lie Still
Sleep Becalmed sufferer with the wound
in the throat
Burning and turning

Sylvia Carlisle-Read

And once below a time I lordly had the trees and leaves

D Jose

Edith Cotton

Lie still, sleep becalmed, hide the mouth in the throat or we shall obey, and ride with you through the drowned

Lisa Ann Tallis

Dave Anthony

Never such seas as any that swamped
the decks of his S.S. Kidwelly bellying
over the bedclothes and jellyfish-
slippery sucking him down salt deep into
the Davy dank where the fish come biting
out and nibble him down to his wishbone
and the long drowned nuzzle up to him

Sun the father his quiver full of the
Infants of pure fire.

Tracey Dobson

Barbara Dudley

On no work of words for three lean
months in the bloody Belly of the
rich year and the big purse of my
body I bitterly take to task my
poverty and craft:

D Jose

Jack Thorpe

34

Mair Johnson

Rita Williams

June Camm

Roy Kneath

I wish I was a baby
and look up mothers skirt
and see the Cocket tunnel
Where daddy drives his Engine

Raymond Fry

In the poles of the year
When black birds died like priests in the cloaked hedge row
And over the cloth of counties the far hills rode near,
Under the one leaved trees ran a scarecrow of snow
And fast through the drifts of the thickets antlered like deer.

John Davies

Do not go gentle into that good night

Robert Wyman

Unknown

Ursula Calvin-Thomas

Inside the large collage:

> Oh as I was young and easy in the mercy of his means
> Time held me green and dying
> Though I sang in my chains like the sea
> DYLAN THOMAS

DYLAN
THOMAS
POET
1914-1953
was born in
this house

~~ tells the windy weather in the cock.

~~ Some let me make you of the meadow's signs.

Anne Llewellyn

~~ AN ANCIENT UNCERTAIN BODY WHO WORE A
HAT WITH CHERRIES ~~ CARRYING A PHOTOGRAPH ALBUM
AND THE CUTGLASS FRUIT BOWL FROM THE FRONT ROOM.
FROM: "HOLIDAY MEMORY".

Lorna Thornton

altarwise by owl-light

Jackie Davies

Diane Darrell

The sun was red the moon was grey The earth and sky were as two mountains meeting

All the Christmases roll down the hill towards the Welsh speaking sea, Like a cold and headlong moon bundling down the sky......

Alan Warnham

Alex Evans

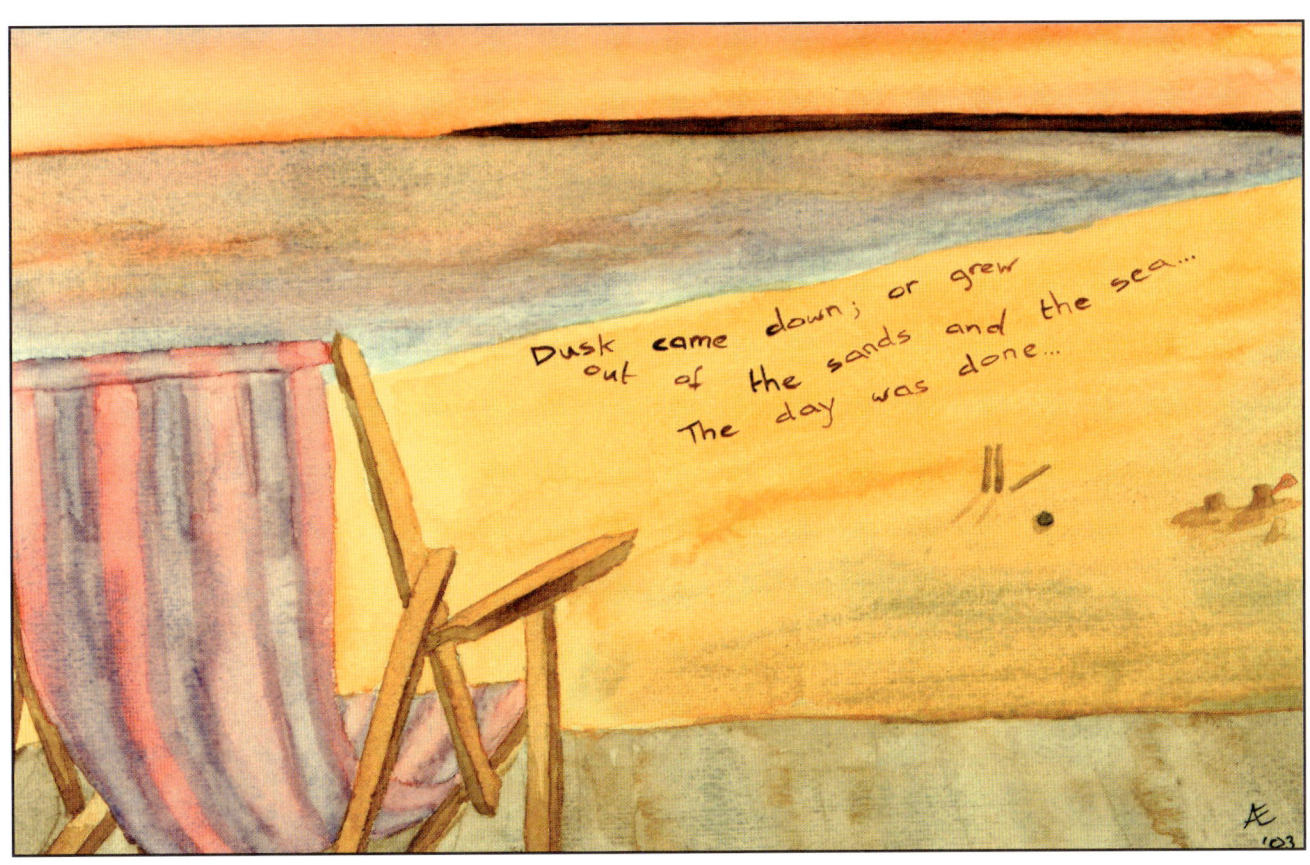

Dusk came down; or grew
out of the sands and the sea...
The day was done...

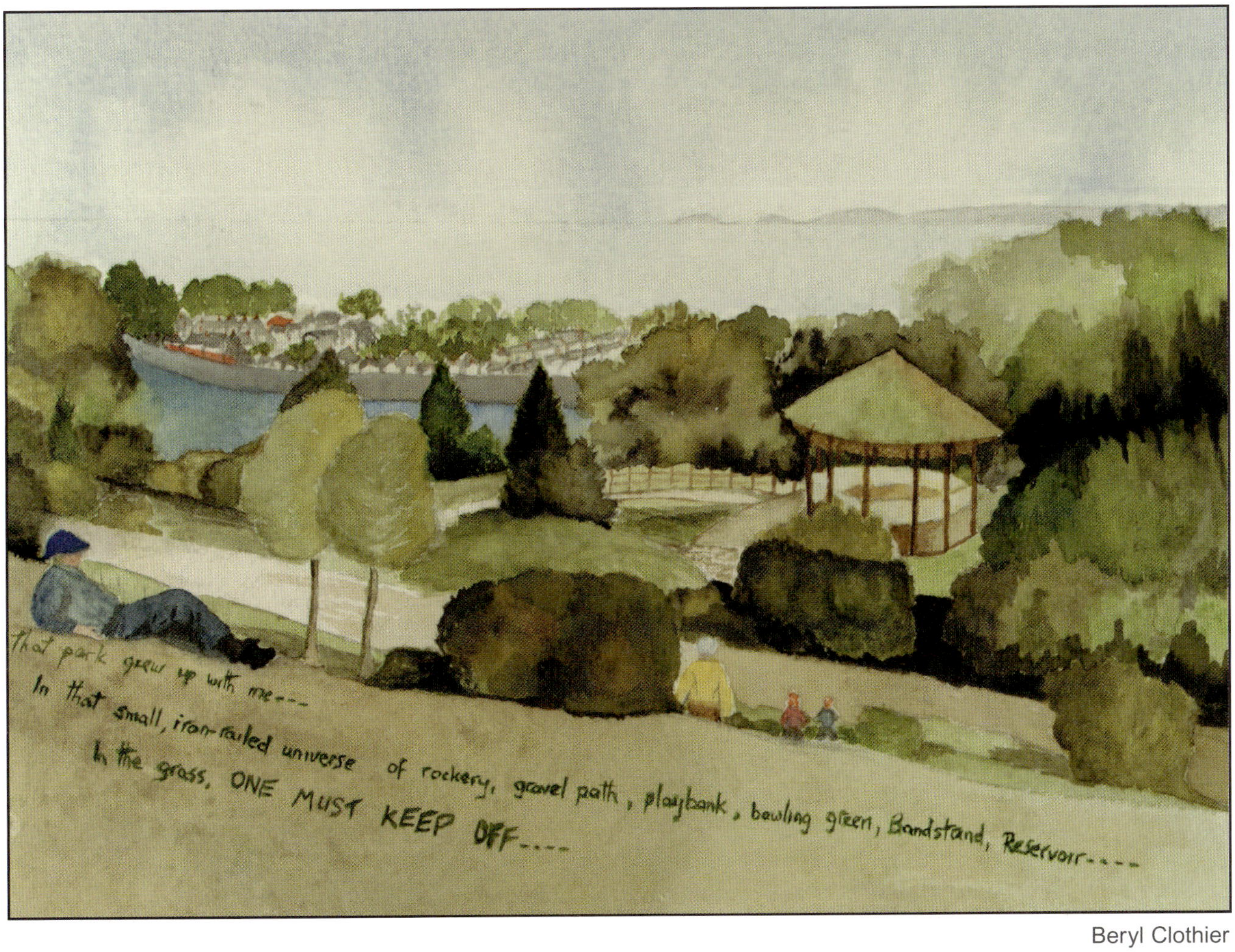
That park grew up with me---
In that small, iron-railed universe of rockery, gravel path, playbank, bowling green, Bandstand, Reservoir----
In the grass, ONE MUST KEEP OFF----

Beryl Clothier

Sam Galoriel

Light breaks where no sun shines; where no sea runs, the waters of the heart push in their tides

Light breaks where no sun shines; where no sea runs, the waters of the heart push in their tide

Sian Seabrook

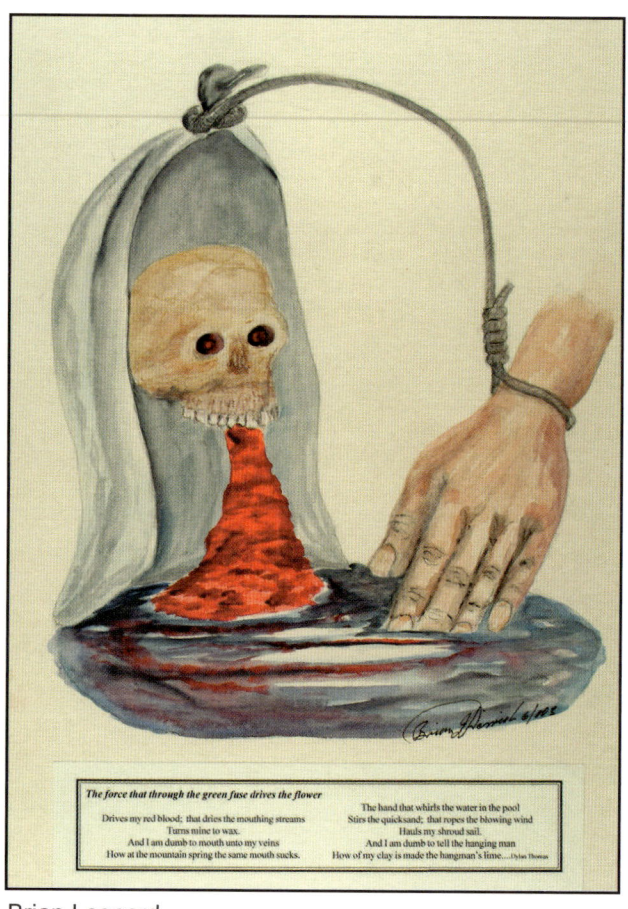

Brian Leonard

42

Natasha Smith

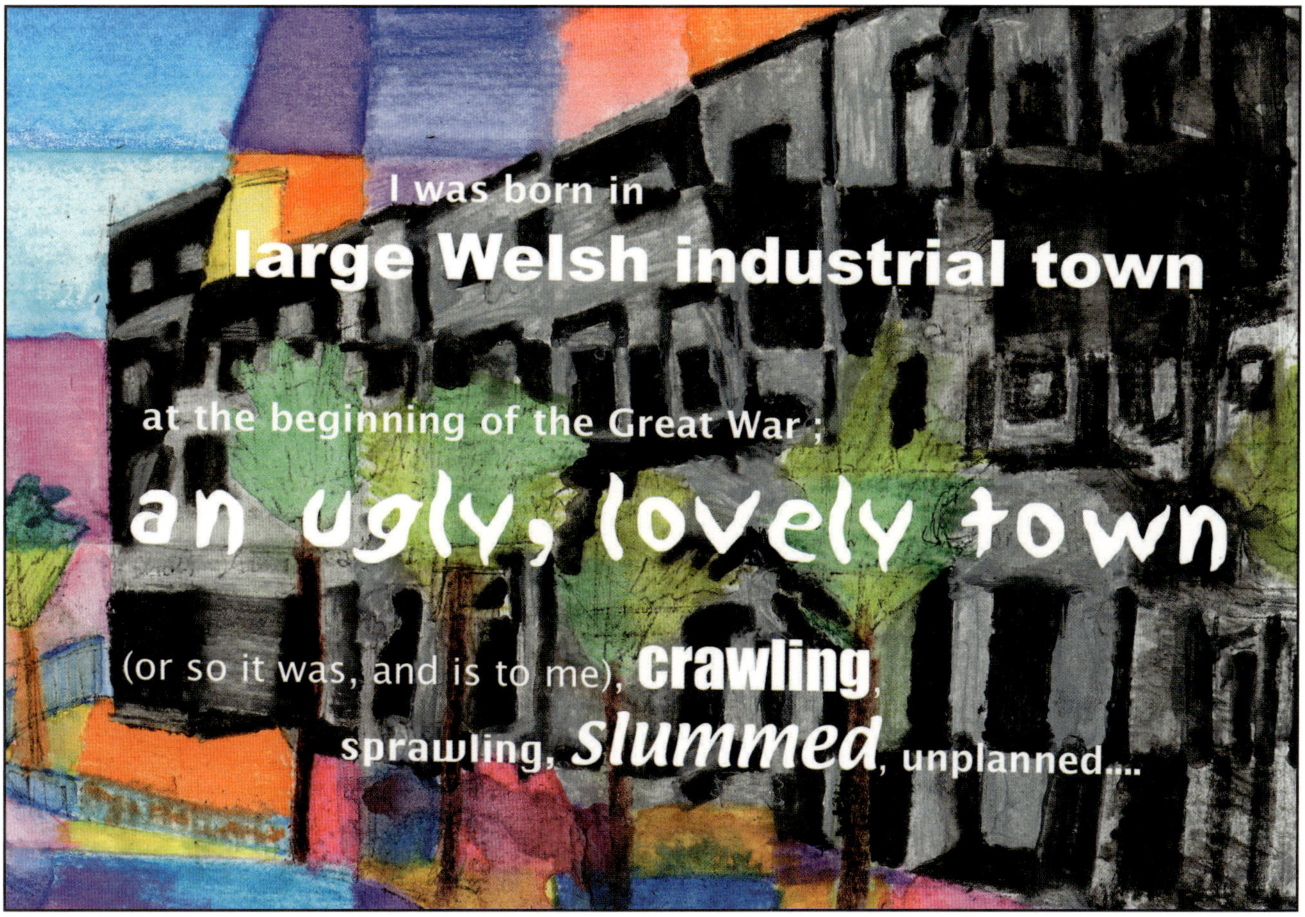

I was born in
large Welsh industrial town

at the beginning of the Great War ;

an ugly, lovely town

(or so it was, and is to me), **crawling**,
sprawling, *slummed*, unplanned....

We can still laugh with the
DEAD

Jemma Ewers

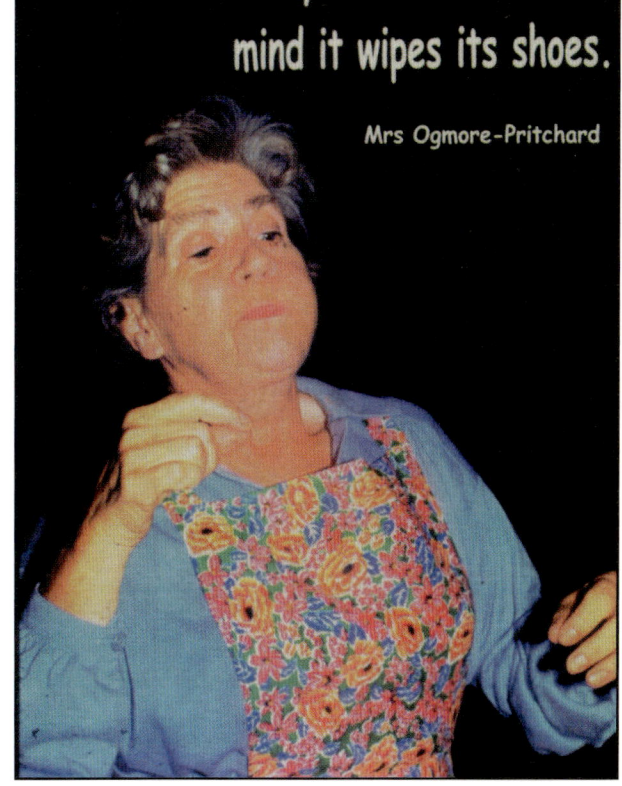

And before you let the sun in,
mind it wipes its shoes.

Mrs Ogmore-Pritchard

Roy Kneath

Brian Leonard

Ursula Calvin-Thomas

August Bank Holidays A tune on an ice-cream cornet
A Slap of Sea a tickle of sand. A Fan fare of sunshades
opening A wince and whimsy of bathers dancing in
deceptive water

Lorna Thornton

45

Nick Doyle

G Homer

Diane Darrell

Nick Doyle

Janet Thomas

Anne Llewellyn

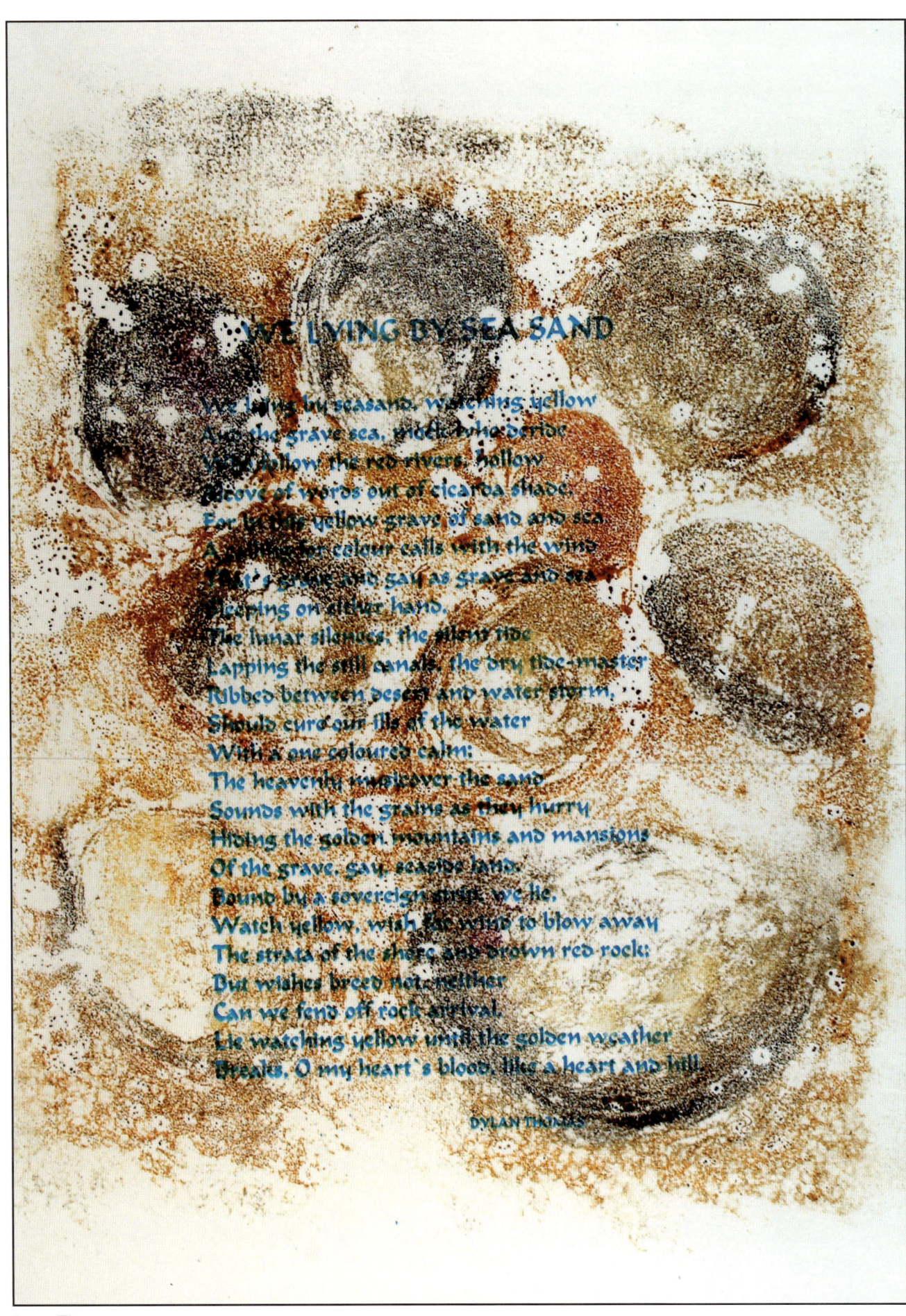

WE LYING BY SEA SAND

We lying by seasand, watching yellow
And the grave sea, mock who deride
With yellow the red rivers, hollow
Groove of words out of cicada shade,
For in this yellow grave of sand and sea
A calling for colour calls with the wind
That's grave and gay as grave and sea
Sleeping on either hand.
The lunar silences, the silent tide
Lapping the still canals, the dry tide-master
Ribbed between desert and water storm,
Should cure our ills of the water
With a one coloured calm;
The heavenly music over the sand
Sounds with the grains as they hurry
Hiding the golden mountains and mansions
Of the grave, gay, seaside land.
Bound by a sovereign strip, we lie,
Watch yellow, wish for wind to blow away
The strata of the shore and drown red rock;
But wishes breed not, neither
Can we fend off rock arrival,
Lie watching yellow until the golden weather
Breaks, O my heart's blood, like a heart and hill.

DYLAN THOMAS

Irene Thomas

48

Ann Legg

As we climbed home, up the gas lit hill, to the still homes .... we heard the music die and the voices drift like sand ...

A E. Legg 03.

Every morning when I wake,
Dear Lord, a little prayer I make,
O please to keep Thy lovely eye
On all poor creatures born to die.

And every evening at sundown
I ask a blessing on the town,
For whether we last the night or no
I'm sure is always touch-and-go.

We are not wholly bad or good
Who live our lives under Milk Wood,
And Thou, I am sure wilt be the first
To see our best side, not our worst.

O let us see another day!
Bless us all this night, I pray,
And to the sun we all will bow
And say good-bye—but just for now!

Dave Anthony

Joyce Powell

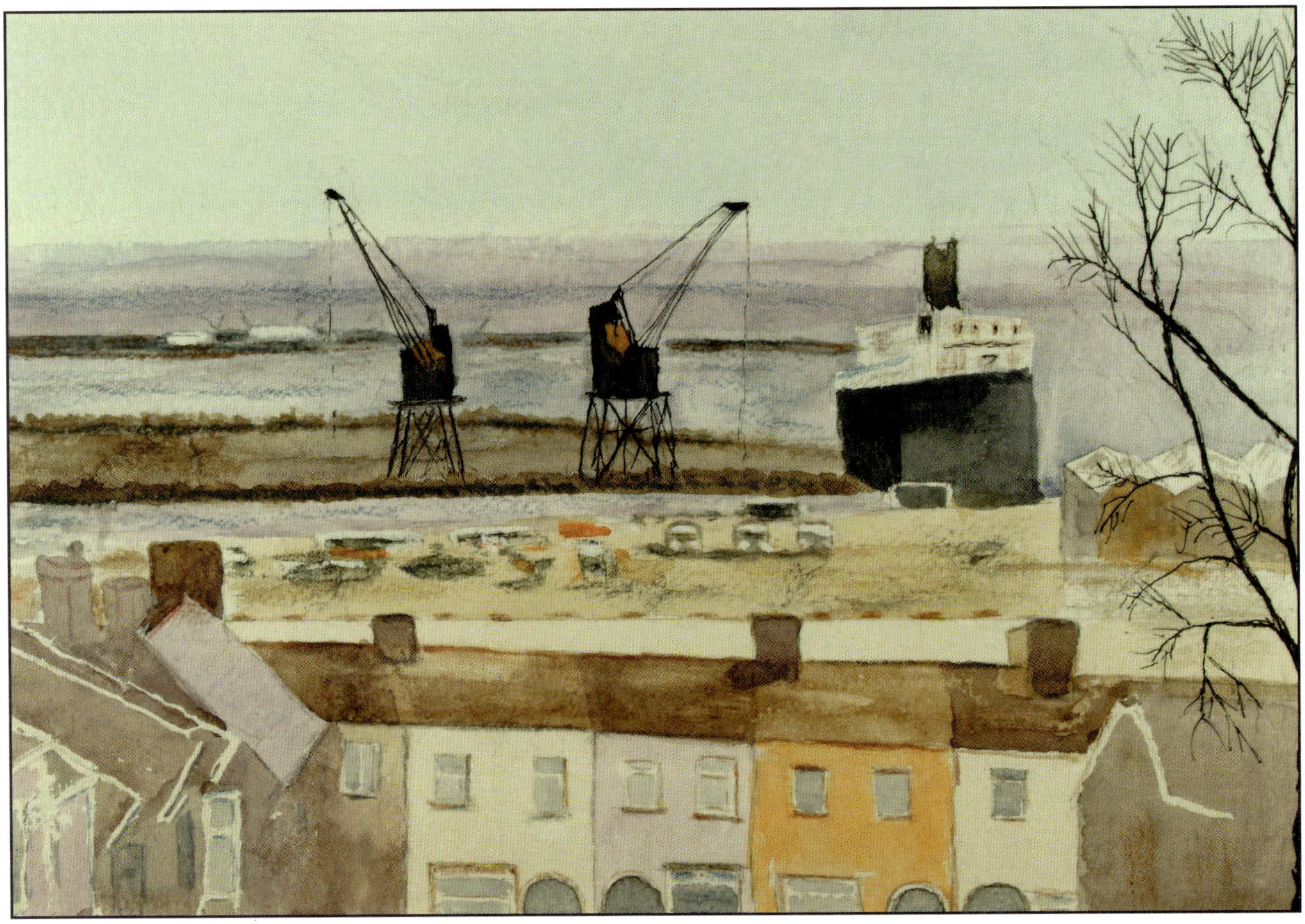

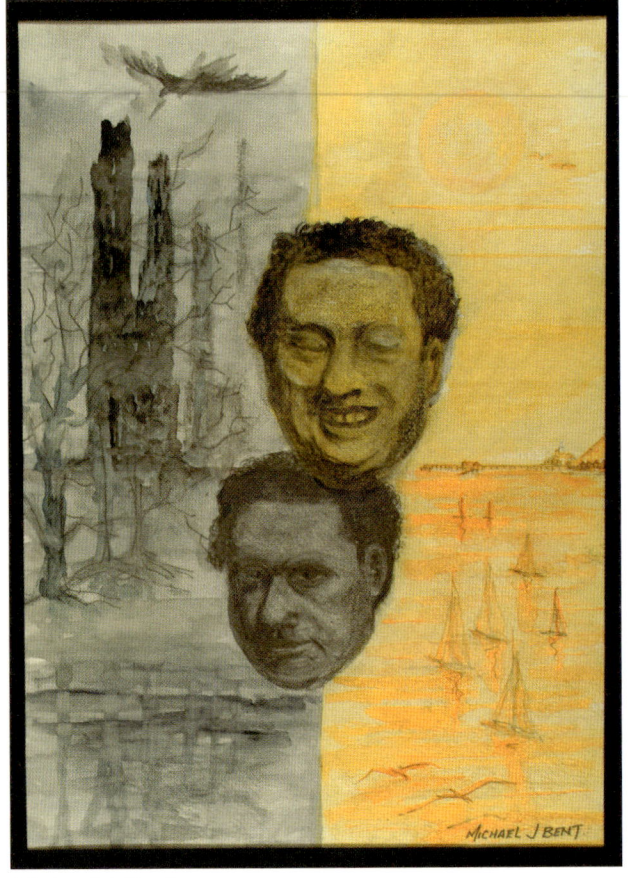

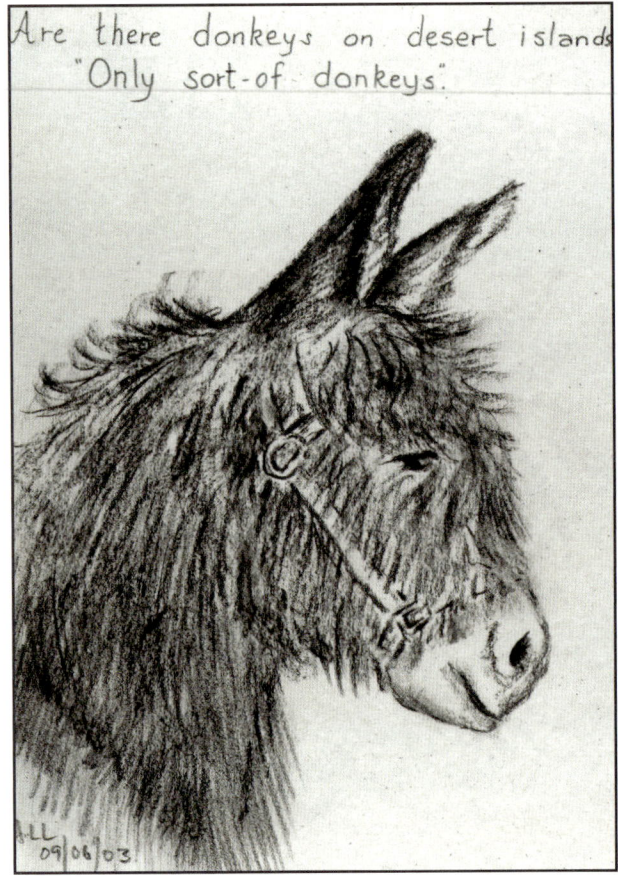

Are there donkeys on desert islands
"Only sort-of donkeys".
09/06/03

Anne Llewellyn

MICHAEL J BENT

Michael J Bent

The Spire Cranes

Its statue is an aviary.

Joyce Powell

in country sleep

Jackie Davies

ESPECIALLY WHEN OCTOBER WIND
WITH FROSTY FINGERS PUNISHES MY HAIR

CAUGHT BY THE CRABBING SUN I WALK ON FIRE
AND CAST A SHADOW CRAB UPON THE LAND

Michael J Bent

53

Maria

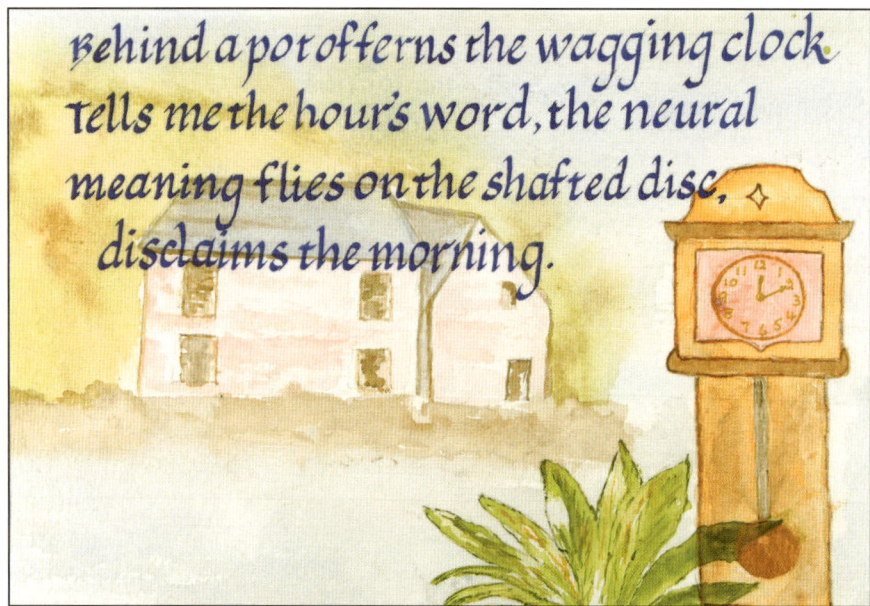

Brian Leonard

Alex Evans

Kelly Diane Lloyd

Brian Derrick

Irene Thomas

RAGE, RAGE

against the

DO NOT go

dying of the light.

gentle

into that good night,

old age should burn and rave

at close of day;

Kathryn Vickery

Brian Gaylor

And I rose
In rainy autumn
And walked abroad in a shower of all my days

laying

my

ghost

in

metal

Lucy Llewellyn

G Tooth

The Force that through the green fuse drives the flower

Michael J Bent

Holly Diment

Vicki Mills

Sian Jones

Jackie Davies

Brian Derrick

Lorna Thornton

Edith Cotton

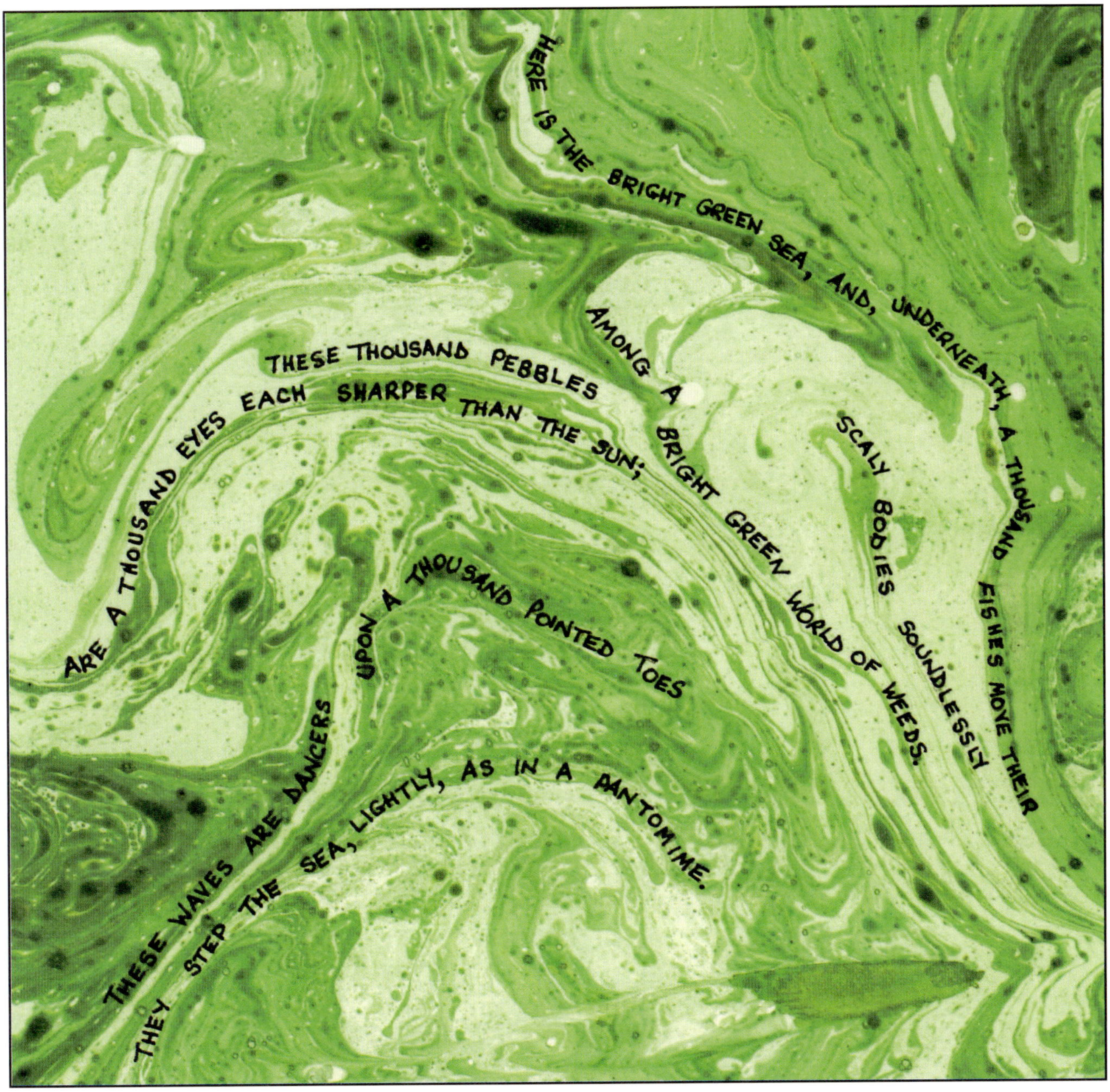

HERE IS THE BRIGHT GREEN SEA, AND, UNDERNEATH, A THOUSAND

THESE THOUSAND PEBBLES

AMONG A BRIGHT GREEN WORLD OF WEEDS.

THESE WAVES ARE DANCERS

ARE A THOUSAND EYES EACH SHARPER THAN THE SUN;

SCALY BODIES SOUNDLESSLY

FISHES MOVE THEIR

UPON A THOUSAND POINTED TOES

THEY STEP THE SEA, LIGHTLY, AS IN A PANTOMIME.

Rho undydd eto, Arglwydd da,
A'th fendith hwyrol caniatâ!
Ac wrth yr haul sy'n mynd am sbel
Cawn ddweud nos da,
heb ddweud

FFAR WEL

The Judith Porch group

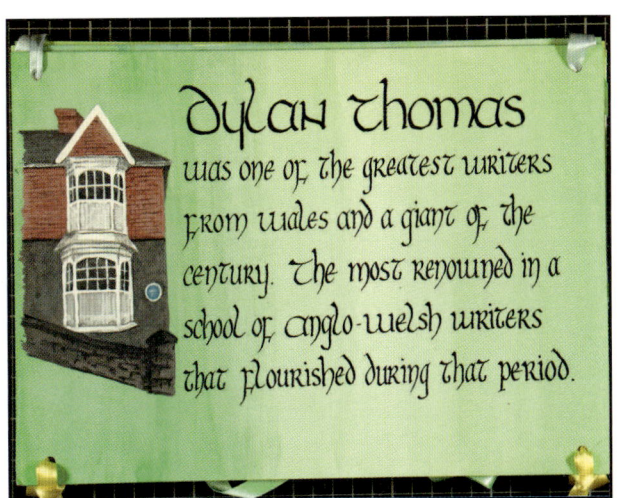

dylan thomas was one of the greatest writers from wales and a giant of the century. The most renowned in a school of anglo-welsh writers that flourished during that period.

The Judith Porch group

AND THE KNOCK OF SAILING BOATS ON NET WEBBED WALL
MYSELF TO SET FOOT------

----- ITS HORNS THROUGH MIST AND THE CASTLE
BROWN AS OWLS
BUT-----

Michael J Bent

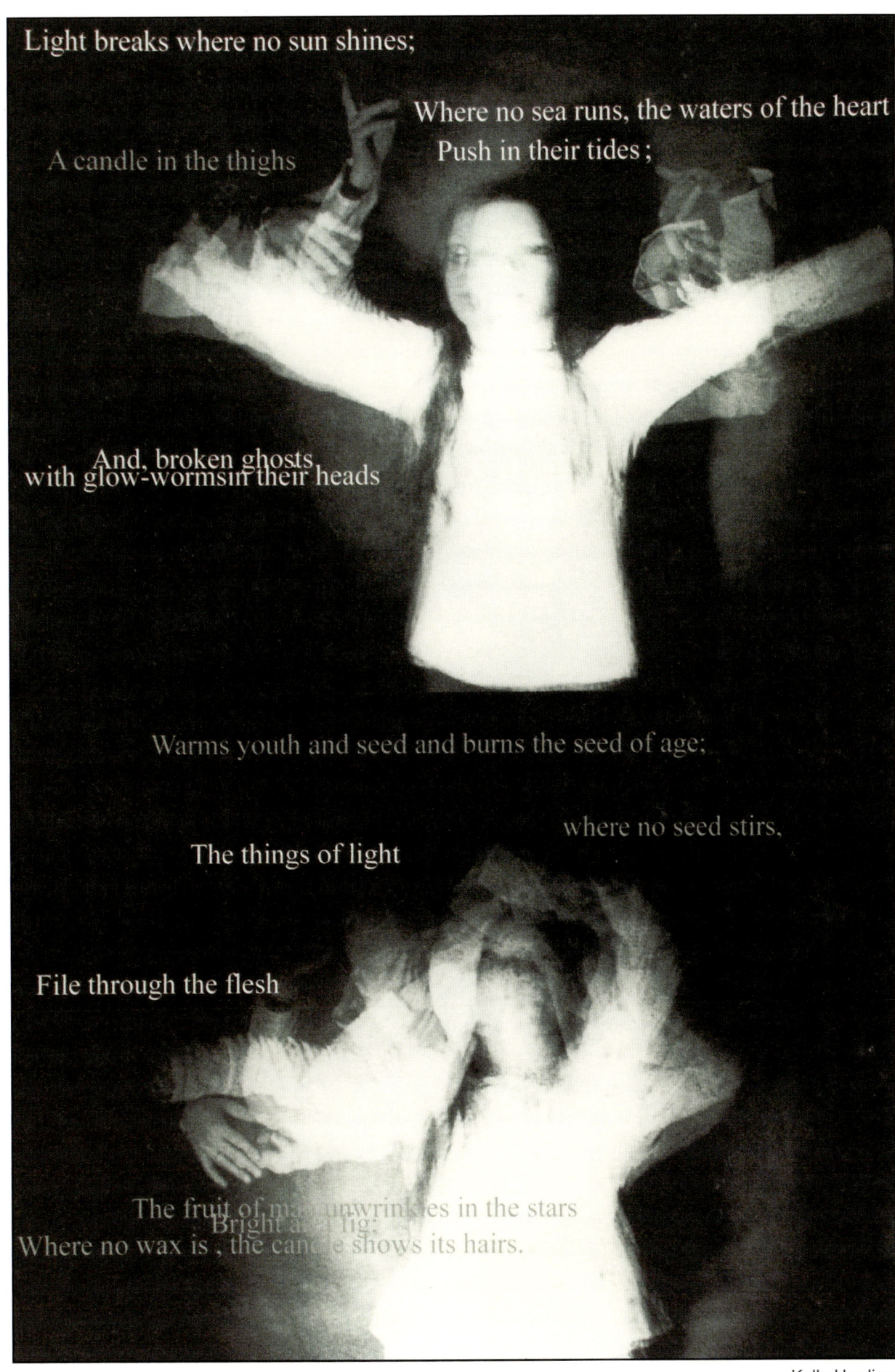

Light breaks where no sun shines;

Where no sea runs, the waters of the heart
Push in their tides;

A candle in the thighs

And, broken ghosts
with glow-worms in their heads

Warms youth and seed and burns the seed of age;

where no seed stirs,

The things of light

File through the flesh

The fruit of man unwrinkles in the stars
Bright as a fig;
Where no wax is, the candle shows its hairs.

Kelly Harding

Sylvia Carlisle-Read

Mair Johnson

And I will build

my liquid world

Justine Gardner

Joe Harris

Rita Williams

Haley Szymonski

Joe Harris

Kayleigh Collins

65

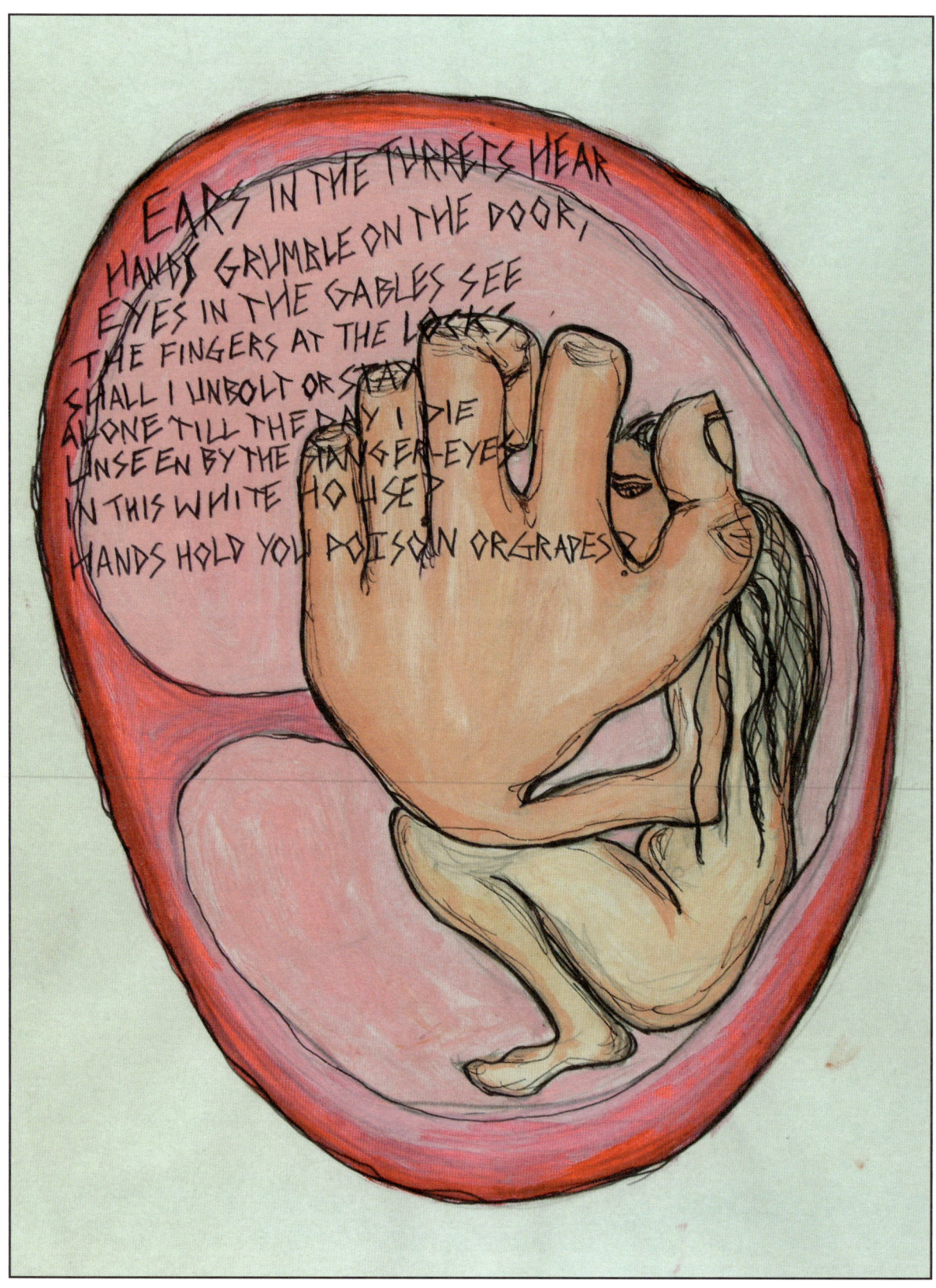

Frances Stokes

Haley Szymonski

Michael J Bent

Eleanor Pugh

June Camm

Friendship House Group

Dusk is drowned for
ever until tomorrow

Philip Thomas

Lorna Thornton

...the falling alleys and brick lanes

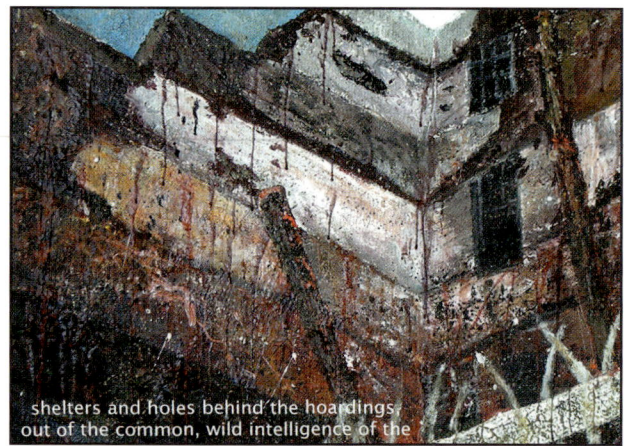

shelters and holes behind the hoardings,
out of the common, wild intelligence of the

Sarah Thomas

kirsty Griffiths

DYLAN
THOMAS
1914 – 53

Jean Guard

Friendship House Group

Lorna Thornton

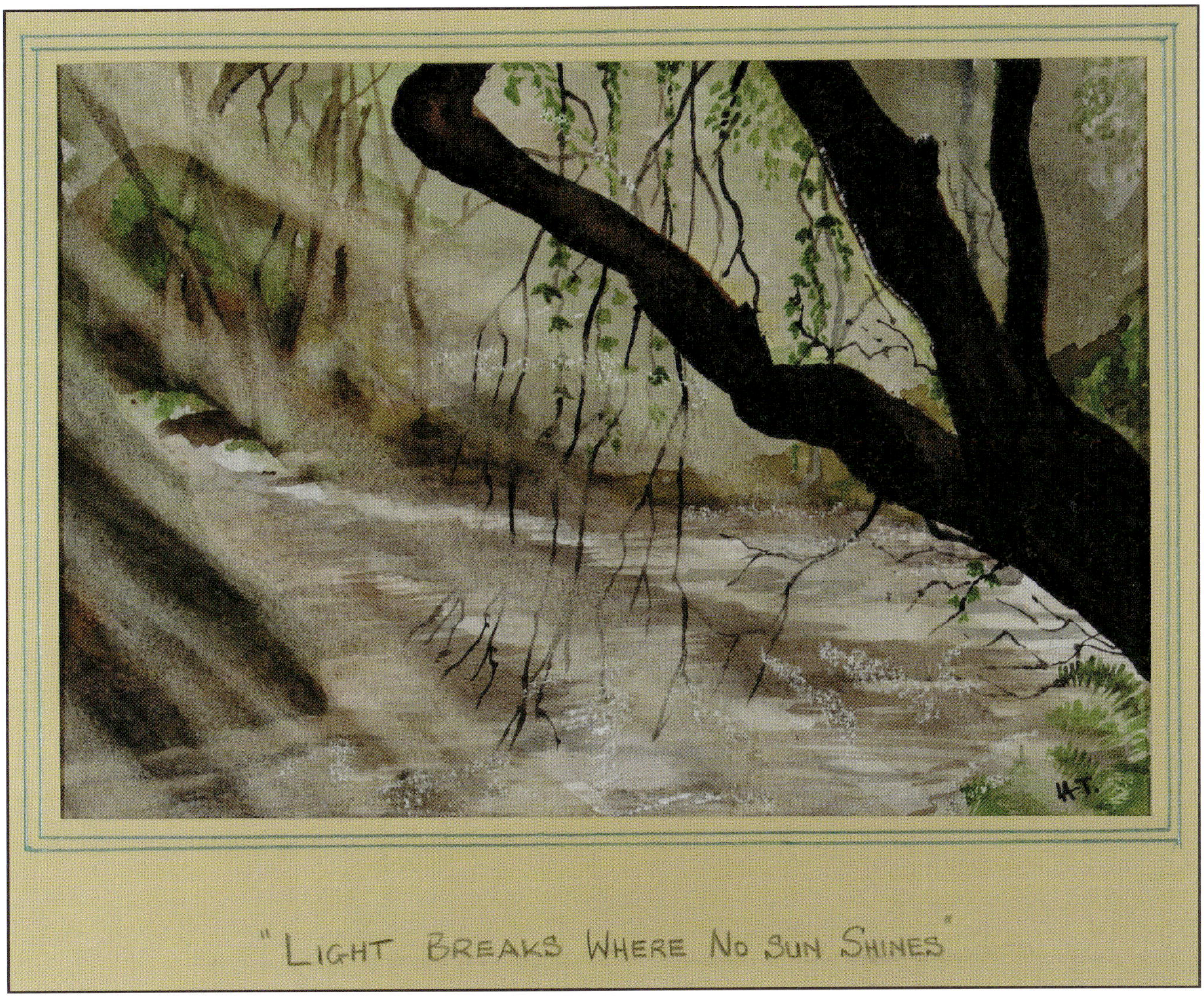
"Light Breaks Where No Sun Shines"

Here
is
the
bright
green
sea

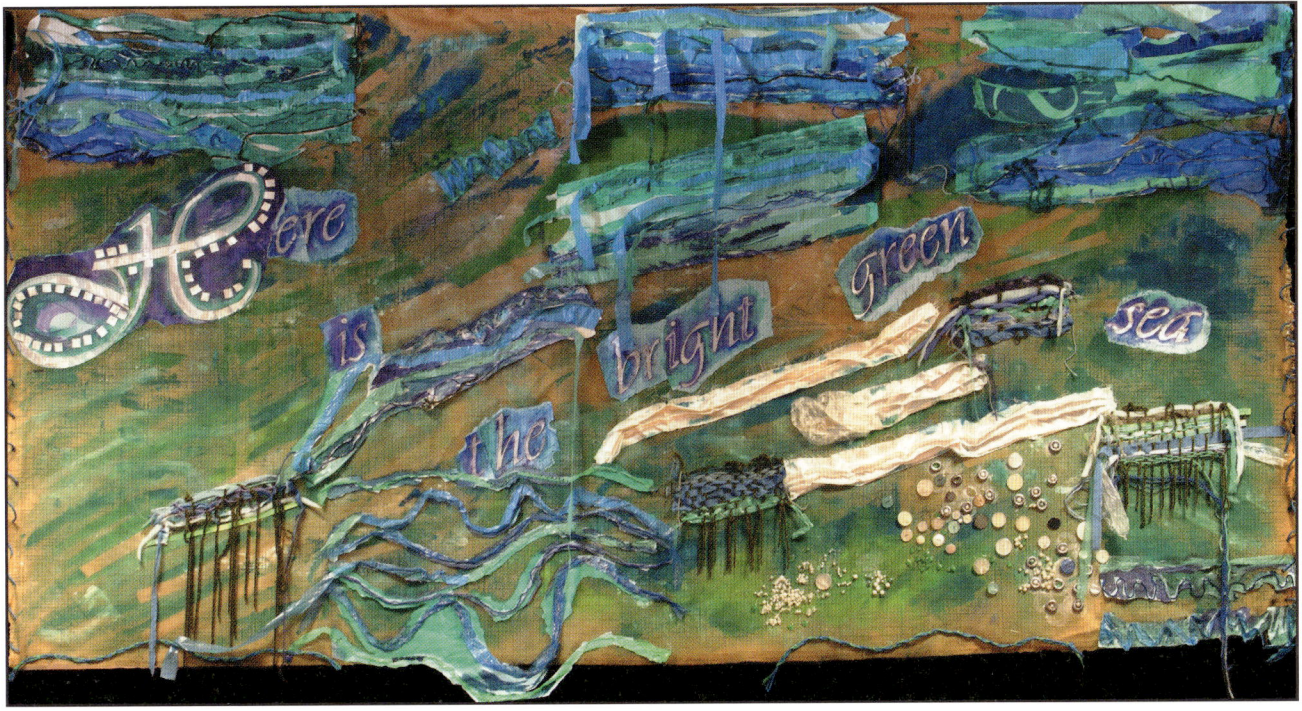

The Janet Evans Group

Her garden
blooms with iris
and it seems
The moons are
white flames like
the moons
in dreams

Eleanor Pugh

Miriam Evans

Mair Johnson

Do not go gentle into that
Though wise men at their end know
And you my father there on the
Rage, rage against the

good night.
dark is right
on the sad height
dying of the light

The Judith Porch Group

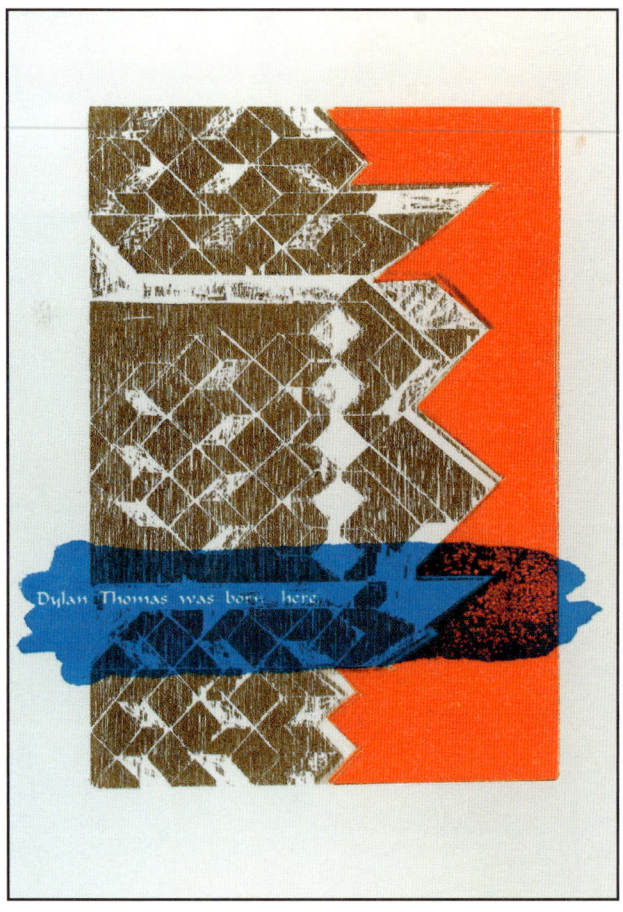

Dylan Thomas was born here.

D Jose

Ruth Parmiter

By the seas side hear
the dark-vowelled birds

To glow after
the god stoning night

Tracey Dobson

At home, in the warm living-room

Sam Turner

73

Sylvia Carlisle-Read

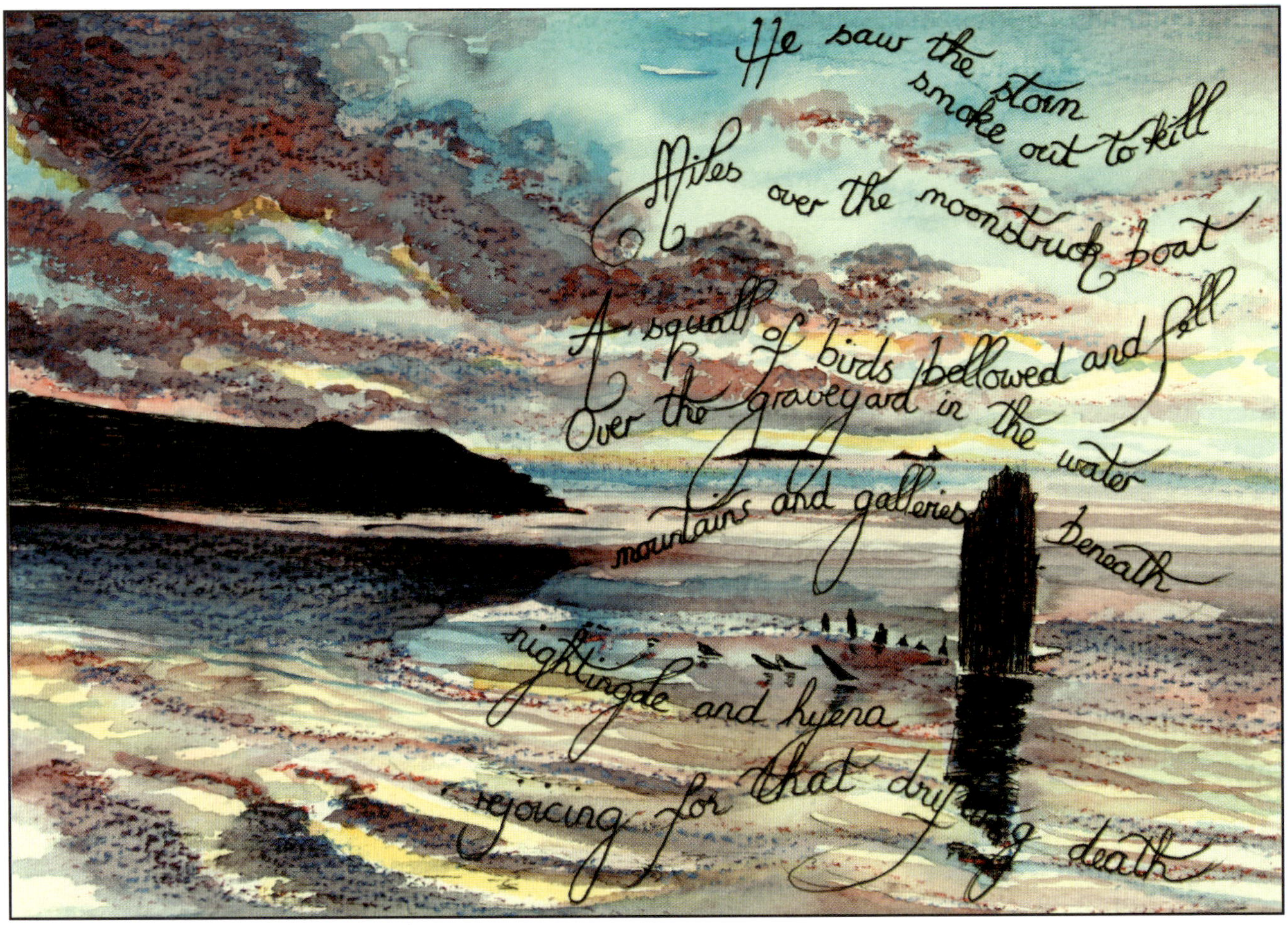
He saw the storm
smoke out to kill
Miles over the moonstruck boat
A squall of birds bellowed and fell
Over the graveyard in the water
mountains and galleries beneath
nightingale and hyena
rejoicing for that dri g death

And over the sea wet church the size of a snail

Hilary Ferris

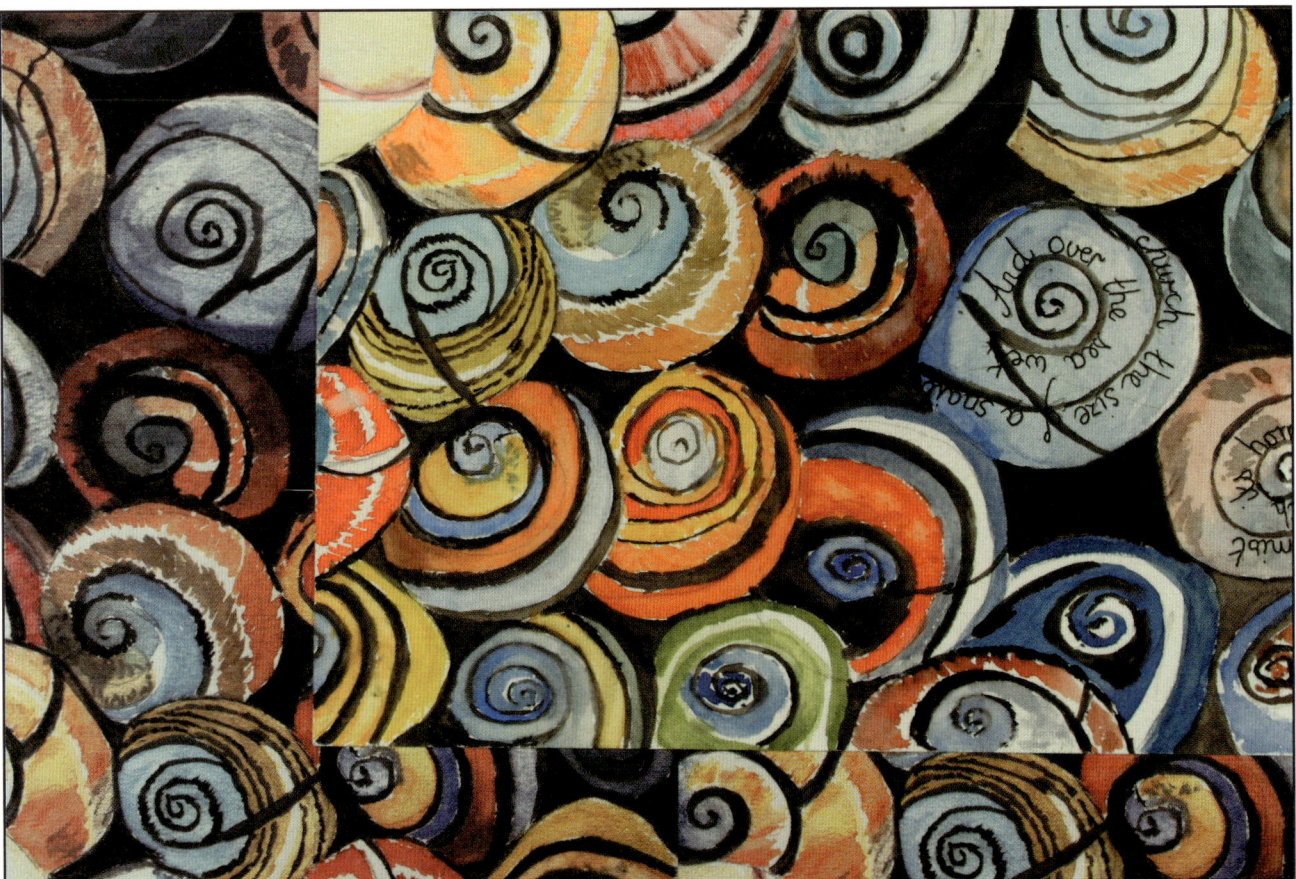

katie James-Flatt

Rita Williams

Brian Derrick

Joyce Powell

Eirwen Jones

Sylvia Carlisle-Read

Rita Ford

77

Shall Gods Be Said to Thump The Clouds

Shall gods be said to thump the clouds
When clouds are cursed by thunder,
Be said to weep when weather howls?
Shall rainbows be their tunics' colour?

When it is rain where are the gods?
Shall it be said they sprinkle water
From garden cans, or free the floods?

Shall it be said that, venuswise,
An old god's dugs are pressed and pricked,
The wet night scolds me like a nurse?

Miriam Evans

Woke to my hearing from harbour

And the knocking of sailing boats on the net webbed wall.

Michael J Bent

Rita Williams

Brian Leonard

Lorna Thornton

80

Alan Warnham

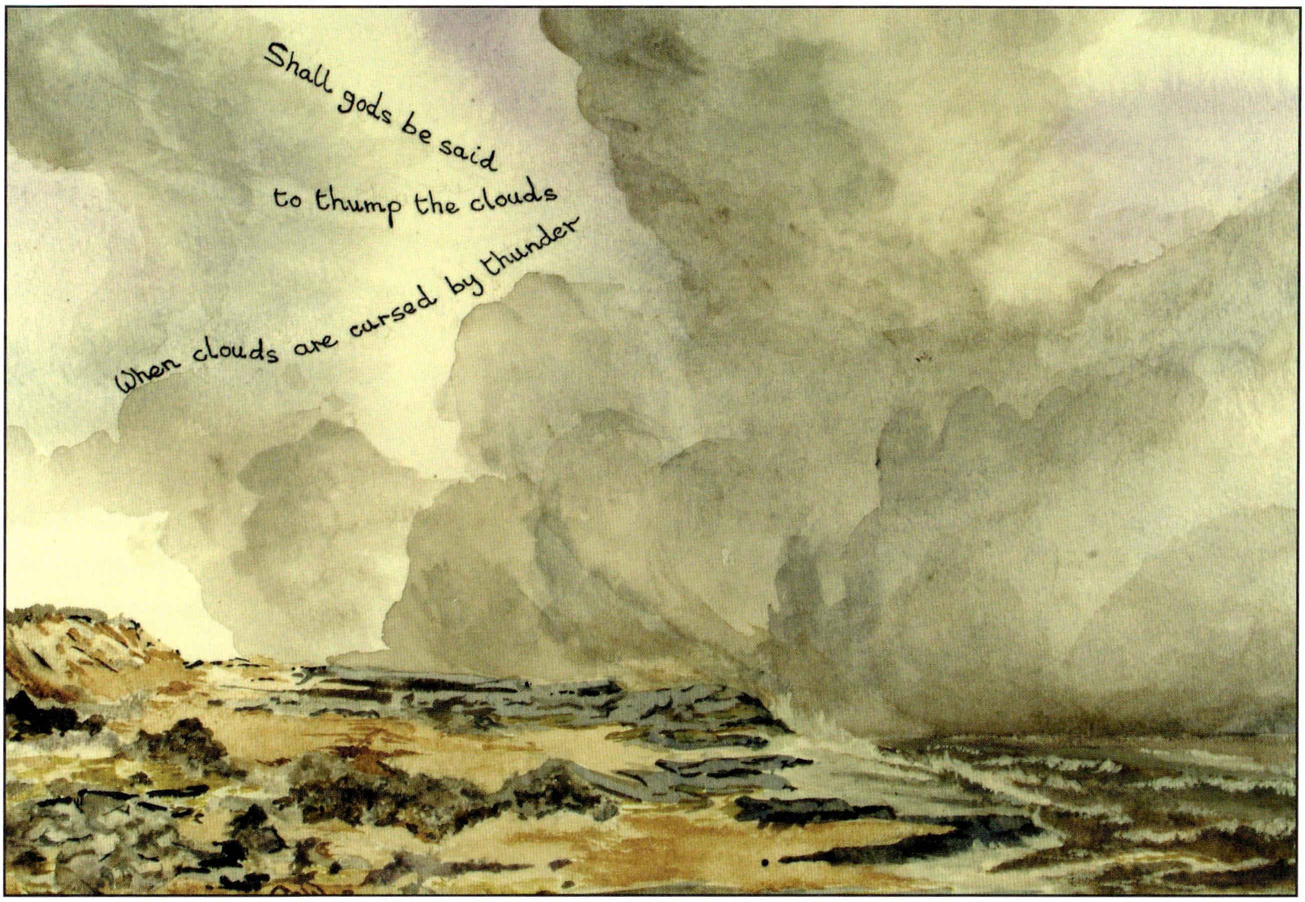
Shall gods be said
to thump the clouds
When clouds are cursed by thunder

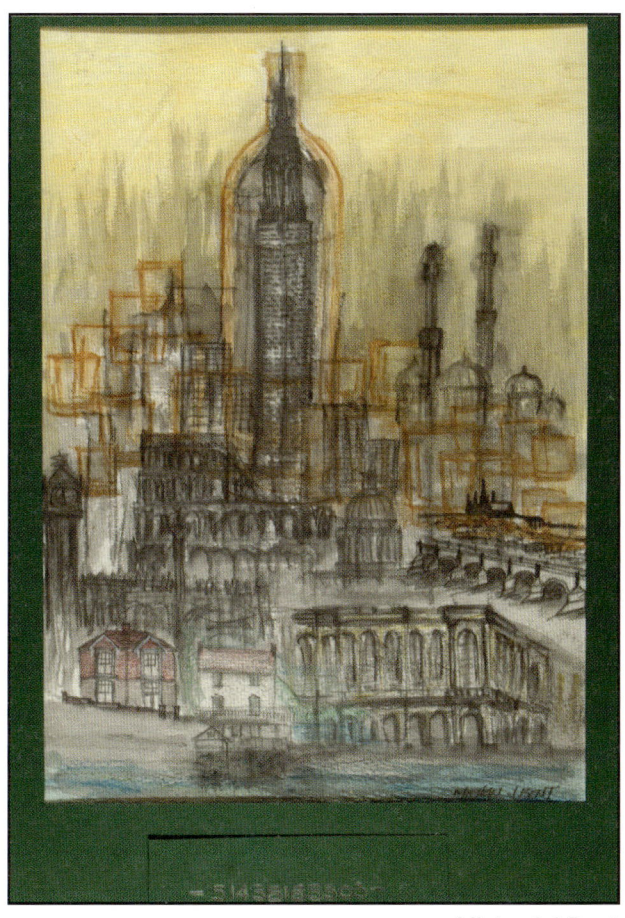

Michael J Bent

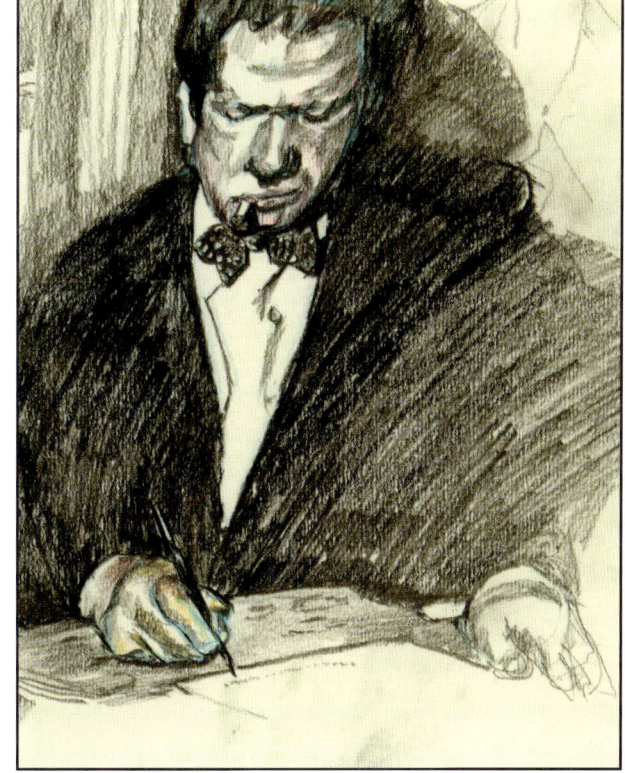

Brian Leonard

Ursula Calvin-Thomas

Anthony Rowlands

Michael J Bent

BERYL CLOTHIER
Alan Warnham

Shall gods be said to thump the clouds when clouds are cursed by thunder,

Be said to weep when weather howls?

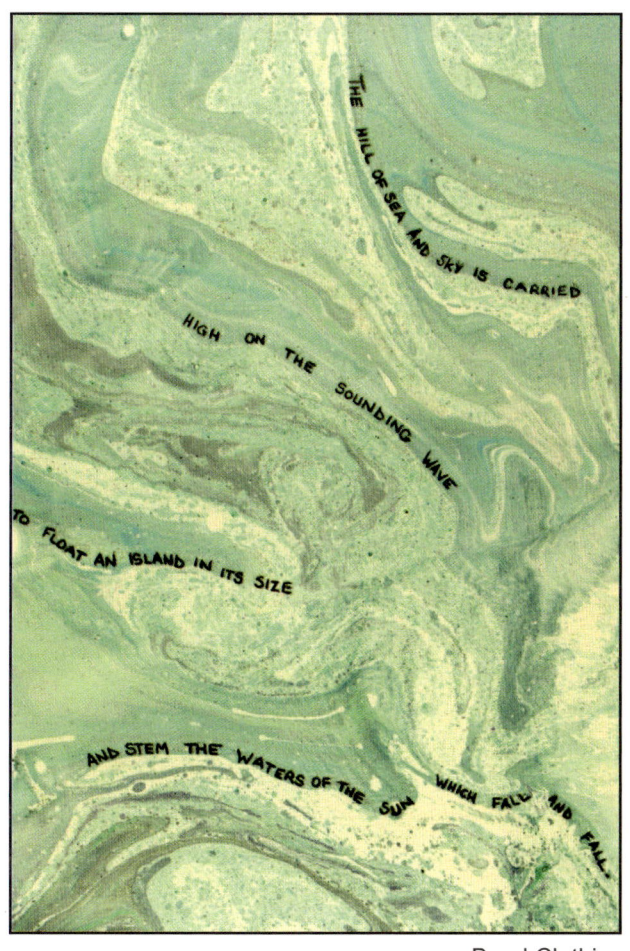

THE HILL OF SEA AND SKY IS CARRIED

HIGH ON THE SOUNDING WAVE

TO FLOAT AN ISLAND IN ITS SIZE

AND STEM THE WATERS OF THE SUN WHICH FALL AND FALL

Beryl Clothier
LINDA THORNTON

Brian Leonard

Lorna Thornton

Hilary Ferris

Eleanor Pugh

Lorna Thornton

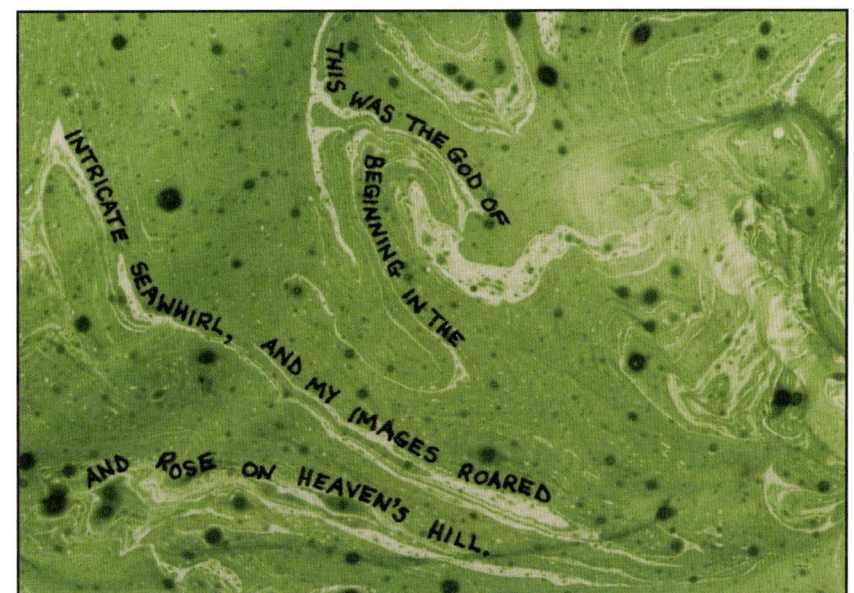

THIS WAS THE GOD OF BEGINNING IN THE INTRICATE SEAWHIRL, AND MY IMAGES ROARED AND ROSE ON HEAVEN'S HILL.

Judith Roeder

That her loving, unfriendly limbs
Would plunge my betrayal from sheet to sky

Edith Cotton

THE HAWK ON FIRE HANGS STILL

THE HOLY STALKING HERON

OVER SIR JOHNS HILL

E.Cotton 2003

85

Sylvia Carlisle-Read

AS TARRED WITH BLOOD
AS THE BRIGHT HORNS
WEPT

In my craft or sullen art. In my craft or sullen art Exercised in the still night when only the moon rages and lovers

Brian Leonard

私は倉川造牛を地球上でスカウイングたせさ

Lorna Thornton

The heart is drained that, spelling in the scurry Of chemic blood, warned of the coming fury
By the sea's side hear the dark- vowelled birds

Brian Derrick